the art of STAYING OFF DEAD-END STREETS

Richard W. De Haan
and
Herbert Vander Lugt

Published by

VICTOR BOOKS

a division of SP Publications, Inc.
WHEATON, ILLINOIS 60187

Scripture quotations in this book are from *The New Scofield Reference Bible*, © 1967 by the Delegates of the Oxford University Press, Inc., New York. Used by permission.

Library of Congress Catalog Card Number: 74-79163
ISBN 0-88207-710-4

VICTOR BOOKS
A division of SP Publications, Inc.
P.O. Box 1825 • Wheaton, Illinois 60187

Contents

Preface

The book of Ecclesiastes is not easy to understand, but it contains a tremendous message of instruction and encouragement for God's people who live in troubled times. The inspired author faces life as it is and demonstrates the total failure of every human philosophy to answer the problems of existence. He portrays the highest goals of the natural man, and shows how they lead to dissatisfaction and emptiness when pursued as ends in themselves. He gives practical counsel to the bewildered and insists that true happiness is found only when one reveres and obeys God. The Preacher was truly a man of faith!

Since very little has been written on Ecclesiastes, except rather technical commentaries, we are happy to present a work designed for the general Christian public. We therefore have not entered into a discussion of authorship or the implications seen by some in the diction and language style of certain sections. We have also avoided the use of terms not readily understood by the man on the street. It has been our purpose to bring the treasures of Ecclesiastes to every reader.

The production of this volume has called for extra effort on the part of all involved. A special word of thanks is in order to Clair Hess, Director of Publications at Radio Bible Class, to Editorial Coordinator David Egner, and to Lois Weber who typed the manuscript.

We pray that God will use this book to the instruction and edification of His own and to the salvation of many people who do not know the Lord Jesus Christ as Saviour.

Richard W. De Haan
Herbert Vander Lugt

A Map
for the Maze

One of my friends told me he was puzzled when first reading the Book of Ecclesiastes. It contains numerous statements which seem to contradict other passages in the Bible. He cited this example, "For that which befalleth the sons of men befalleth beasts. Even one thing befalleth them: as the one dieth, so dieth the other; yea, they have all one breath, so that a man hath no preeminence above a beast; for all is vanity. All go unto one place; all are of the dust, and all turn to dust again. Who knoweth the spirit of man that goeth upward, and the spirit of the beast that goeth downward to the earth?" (Ecc. 3:19-21)

How can this assertion that man and beast have the same fate after death be harmonized with the many declarations of the Bible that men, created in the image and likeness of God, do not stop existing when they die? The Scriptures clearly teach that all people will be resurrected, judged, and go either into eternal blessing or everlasting punishment.

A study of this passage (chapter 6 will treat it in

detail) reveals that Solomon made these observations when he was struggling with the problems of existence. Relying on his own wisdom instead of God's, the Preacher was troubled by the idea that maybe God allows men to die in such a humiliating manner to teach us that we are nothing more than animals.

Many similar apparent contradictions to the basic tenets of the Christian faith occur in Ecclesiastes. Yet this book is in our Bibles, and must be looked upon as inspired of God. It was universally recognized as belonging to Holy Writ long before Jesus Christ came to earth, and its acceptance is virtually unquestioned. Furthermore, a careful study of its pages will provide valuable guidance and counsel to God's people in these difficult days. Its treasures will give unexpected help to every sincere believer.

The Key to Its Riches

We need a key to unlock the meaning of the many beneficial statements in this book. A number of Bible scholars believe it is found in the final chapter, where the Preacher speaks of *goads* and *nails*. "The words of the wise are like goads, and like nails fastened by the masters of assemblies, which are given by one Shepherd" (Ecc. 12:11).

The translation of Ecclesiastes 12:11 in the King James Version does not clearly present the distinction between "goads" and "nails" which is so important to the understanding of this book. A better rendering is: "The words of the wise are like goads; and the collected sayings are like fastened nails—they come from one Shepherd."

Hebrew writing, especially that of a poetic nature, is often marked by a feature called parallelism. Two lines occur in tandem, and the second is (1) a *repetition* of the thought of the first line in different words, or (2) an *amplification* of it, or (3) the expression of a *contrasting* idea. Most scholars today reject any translation of Ecclesiastes 12:11 which fails to recognize the occurrence of a parallel construction. Almost all agree, therefore, that the phrase "masters of assemblies" is not the best rendering of this verse.

The parallel ideas of Ecclesiastes 12:11 are as follows: "The *words* of the wise are like goads; the *collected sayings* are like well-fastened nails."

This is an instance of the third alternative of parallelism, a contrast. It occurs between the *words* which are like goads and the *collected sayings* which are like nails firmly fixed. The goads are easily determined as the wisdom of man—his best thoughts as he confronts life's problems. The nails are more difficult to identify. It is our contention that the fastened nails are the "collected sayings" (not "masters of assemblies"*) which come from one Shepherd. In other words, the nails are the sacred Scriptures.

Concerning the phrase, "given by one Shepherd," Leupold says, "This can be a reference only to Jahweh, the Shepherd of Israel (Ps. 80:1), who shepherds His people by giving them the pasturage of the Word on which they can at all times richly

---

* H. C. Leupold, in his valuable *Exposition of Ecclesiastes* (Baker Book House, Grand Rapids, Mich.), points out that the Hebrew expression, *ba'ale 'asuppoth,* which literally reads "masters of the collections," did not have this meaning in historical usage. He says it means " 'collected ones,' or 'collected sayings.' . . . In this scheme of things 'masters of assemblies' have no place. They cannot be introduced without bringing in an element that will not fit into the picture. The *words* themselves are under consideration, not 'leaders of synagogues,' as some commentators have translated this expression. From this parallelism it follows that the words 'collected ones' must mean 'collected sayings' in order to agree with 'the words of the wise.' "

feed. From that point of view the choice of the name 'shepherd' (*ro'eh*) is most appropriate. Nor was there anything new about the term. Observe its use in all periods of Israel's history: Genesis 49:24; Psalm 23:1; Isaiah 40:11; Jeremiah 31:10; Ezekiel 34:11-12."

The secret to uncovering the riches of Ecclesiastes is a proper understanding of the goads and nails. Both the goads (the disturbing reflections of men) and the nails (the revelation of God) are recorded here under divine inspiration. A careful study of them will benefit both the layman and church leader as they face squarely the cacophony of ideas confronting the believer today.

Goads and Nails

We must first expand our understanding of goads and explain their purpose. This will help us distinguish between the goad and nail passages in Ecclesiastes.

The people who lived during biblical days were familiar with goads, for they saw them in use every day. The farmer, walking behind a yoke of oxen pulling a plow, always carried a long stick with a sharp point. He used it to keep the animals moving and to control them. These creatures, though powerful and relatively docile, do not respond to verbal commands the way a horse does. Nor are they inclined to move briskly. A goad was necessary, therefore, to prod them into a steady pace, and to turn them left or right.

The nails Solomon mentioned were either long spikes or tent stakes such as might be used today. Driven deeply, they held securely against all onslaughts.

We may contrast the nails and goads of Ecclesiastes in this manner: The *nail* represents stability, solidness, an anchor. The *goad* signifies a sharp sting, arousing a person from lethargy or driving him in a direction he had not intended to take.

We must also recognize Solomon's distinction between the wise and foolish man. The fool lives only for the moment. He refuses to think about the solemn truths which come to everybody's mind from time to time, and makes short-term pleasure his single reason for living. The wise man, however, observes life carefully. He thinks about what he sees and experiences. He asks questions and tries to come to logical conclusions. He seeks long-range satisfaction, and wants his life to count for something.

This serious-minded person is a better citizen than the man who lives only for momentary thrills. But in some ways he also suffers more, for he squarely faces painful truths about life and reflects upon the meaning of pain, death, and eternity. These serious thoughts serve as goads in his life. When he speaks to others of these apprehensions, they also prod the consciences and minds of those who hear, goading them from complacency and self-satisfaction. It hurts for a person to see himself in the futility of the human predicament with no apparent way of escape.

The Goads

I saw goads work effectively in the life of a resident physician named Bob, who went to work in a large city hospital. They began to sting him as soon as he entered this atmosphere of suffering, heartache, and death. He had been reared in a respectable non-Christian home. His parents were well-to-do, and he had always enjoyed comfortable surroundings.

None of his close relatives or friends had died. He was aware of death, but he had never thought about it very much. He had succeeded in pushing all morbid thoughts out of his mind. Like the majority of his fellow students in medical school, he had accepted the hypothesis that everything, including human life, is a product of the evolutionary process.

But now, seeing firsthand the sufferings of flesh-and-blood human beings, he had to confront the full meaning of his own humanity. He was unable to think of men and women in deep pain as mere collections of atoms, or to look upon them as mechanical, unfeeling objects. When he saw people show tender sacrificial love toward dear ones enduring great agony, he somehow knew these deep personal expressions were more than mechanical or chemical responses. A myriad of disturbing thoughts raced through his mind. And they stung!

This led him to ponder his own relationships with people. He loved his wife, his small daughter, his parents, and his brother. Was nothing significant or meaningful about his feelings toward them? Ouch! The goad penetrated deeply this time!

He began to wonder about his profession. His folks had sacrificed much to send him to medical school, and he had worked many long hours to succeed. He knew that if he were to be conscientious, his life as a doctor would not be easy. Would the material rewards make up for all the pressures? Besides, if man is nothing more than an accidental step in an evolutionary process, why give all you have to save an individual life? Bob winced in pain as he reflected upon these questions. The goads were digging in more deeply!

While haunted by all this inner turmoil, Bob had

occasion from time to time to meet Christians. They showed remarkable serenity, even under the most difficult circumstances. Some of them shared their faith with him, but he found it hard to accept what they had to say. Day and night his thoughts tormented him. The goads were jabbing him mercilessly! Finally, he accepted the Scriptures and placed his faith in Jesus Christ. Now his heart is filled with deep peace and joy, and he knows how he can truly help others. He had been wise in facing up to life's basic problems, and his thoughts had acted as goads to drive him to the Saviour.

Some people will not let themselves feel the sting of serious introspection. They do not want to threaten their sense of well-being. To escape they may bury themselves in work, or become busy with a thousand special interests. They may lose themselves in the madness of the pleasure-seeking crowd, or relentlessly drive toward the attainment of wealth or fame. Or, they may dodge the goads of reflective thinking by taking drugs, participating in occult practices, or devoting themselves to a manmade religion. A few even accept a philosophy which tells a person that he does not have to carry his thoughts out to their logical conclusions, but that he should simply make believe that life has some kind of purpose or goal. All of these are ways contemporary people sidestep the painful confrontations with the unpleasant realities of human existence. Though they may escape the prod of the goads, they will never find peace with God.

The goads work on the conscience as well as the intellect. The young doctor felt the sting in his *mind,* but a salesman who was recently converted had experienced these painful pricks in his *conscience.* After he was led to the Lord by a member of the Radio Bible Class staff, he said that as a boy he had made a profession of receiving Christ, but that he had only posed as a Christian. He later married a girl who was a devout believer, but he soon stopped attending church and began living for selfish pleasures. He spent more money than he should have, padded his expense account to increase his income, and even began cheating on his wife. It soon became necessary for him to tell one lie after another to stay out of trouble.

He said that during these years he played the role of a happy and successful man, but that in reality he was tormented and miserable. Often, when alone in a motel room, he would visualize the face of his loving, pure, and godly wife, and deep feelings of guilt would sweep over him. Oh, how the goads of conscience stung! Sometimes he would think of his two small children, whom he loved very much. He realized he was betraying them and setting a terrible example, and this too would plunge him into deep remorse. But now that he has been saved, he looks back to those disturbing pangs of conscience with gratitude. He said that he could write a new beatitude: "Blessed are they in whom the goads of conscience speak unceasingly, for they will leave their evil ways and find rest and peace in Christ."

In summary, the goads Solomon includes in Ecclesiastes are the recollections, the concerns, the serious thoughts, and the guilt feelings which arise in the consciousness of one who is willing to face things as they are. Their stings are painful, and do not in themselves provide the answer to man's need. But they bring to light a person's sinfulness and helplessness, and thereby may get him started in the right direction. When he is finally driven to faith in Christ, they have served their purpose.

The Nails

The nails, which we have said refer to long spikes or tent stakes, are the truths that come from God through special revelation. For us today they are found in the Bible, God's Word for all men. When Solomon wrote Ecclesiastes, he had only the five books of Moses, plus Joshua, Judges, probably the books of Samuel, and many of the Psalms, for at that time God was in the process of making Himself and His will known to men.

The author of Hebrews summarized the various ways the Lord has revealed His truth through the centuries when he wrote, "God, who at sundry times and in diverse manners spoke in time past unto the fathers by the prophets, hath in these last days spoken unto us by His Son" (Heb. 1:1-2). The Almighty speaks through creation, providence, and conscience, but Solomon did not have these in mind in Ecclesiastes 12:11 when he referred to the "nails" which he said come from one Shepherd. Nor is that what the writer of Hebrews meant in the verses just quoted. No indeed! Both were referring to the fact that God has revealed Himself, His will, and His redemption directly. He spoke to men such as Moses, David, and the prophets, and they in turn provided a written record of what He said. As we read the Old Testament today, we see how the Lord unfolded to men the great truths they needed to know. Then, when we turn to the New Testament, we are given the climax of God's self-disclosure in the person and work of Jesus Christ—the apex of God's revelation.

The goads, which prick the mind and conscience, are of tremendous value, for they can drive a person away from himself and cause him to lose confidence in his own goodness and wisdom. But that is about all they can do. They must be supplemented by the nails of special revelation, which show him how to be delivered from the guilt of sin, ransomed from its power, and brought into a right relationship with God.

Summary

The Book of Ecclesiastes, written by the inspiration of God, contains many of mankind's most serious reflections. These are not necessarily God's truth, but they stimulate the minds and hearts of men by forcing them to confront the hopelessness which is the logical result of facing life without God. For that reason we must be careful to recognize the "goad" passages when we see them. But the Preacher also gives us many "nails" of divine truth which he learned through God's special revelation. When driven home, these "spikes of truth" give stability to life and bring peace with God. The goads demonstrate that life without God is a dead-end street, while the nails of revelation point the way to everlasting life.

2

Out of the Woods

Many people, especially golfers and fishermen, will tell you that they can find God in nature. Any minister or layman who has invited many people to attend church has encountered a reply that goes something like this: "Oh, I'm not an atheist. I believe in God, but I don't have to go to church to worship. When I drive through the countryside or go fishing, I can feel His presence as I look about and see the beauty of creation. I think I get just as much out of this as other people do out of a service where they sing hymns and hear a sermon from the Bible."

I am not going to claim that everybody benefits a great deal from attending church. Some congregations never hear the Bible expounded. Then, too, many people attend services just because it is the thing to do. They never put their hearts into the song service or prayers, and pay little attention to the sermon. But the person who truly believes in Jesus Christ will realize that you cannot find God in nature if you bypass the Holy Scriptures. An unsaved person will not establish a satisfying relationship with God by going fishing on Sunday. Neither will the Christian, for he knows that he ought to be in church.

The Goads of Natural Revelation

Solomon, the third king of Israel, thought he could ignore the Scriptures which God had given the Jewish nation and find the Lord through nature. He apparently made quite a study of the world about him, for the writer of I Kings makes the following statement about Solomon's proverbs and songs: "He spoke of trees, from the cedar tree that is in Lebanon even unto the hyssop that springeth out of the wall; he spoke also of beasts, and of fowl, and of creeping things, and of fish" (1 Kings 4:33).

Solomon began the book of Ecclesiastes with a review of his experiences. As a young man, he had searched for meaning in life through many avenues. But all of them proved to be dead-end streets. His opening words, therefore, expressed the sense of futility he felt at the end of his quest. "The words of the Preacher, the son of David, king in Jerusalem. Vanity of vanities, saith the Preacher, vanity of vanities; all is vanity. What profit hath a man of all his labor which he taketh under the sun? One generation passeth away, and another generation cometh, but the earth abideth forever" (Ecc. 1:1-4).

His observation of nature first led him to say that the universe is a closed system, and that everything keeps on going without ever getting anywhere. "The sun also riseth, and the sun goeth down, and hasteth to its place where it rose. The wind goeth toward the south, and turneth about unto the north; it whirleth about continually, and the wind returneth again according to its circuits.

All the rivers run into the sea; yet the sea is not full. Unto the place from whence the rivers come, thither they return again" (Ecc. 1:5-7).

Finally, he says that one who reflects upon life and man's experience is overwhelmed with a sense of boredom, because history, like nature, is just a repetition of the same old thing over and over again. The only reason some things seem to be new is because people have short memories, and they move off the scene in rapid succession.

"All things are full of labor; man cannot utter it. The eye is not satisfied with seeing, nor the ear filled with hearing. The thing that hath been, it is that which shall be; and that which is done, is that which shall be done; and there is no new thing under the sun. Is there any thing whereof it may be said, 'See, this is new'? It hath been already of old time, which was before us. There is no remembrance of former things; neither shall there be any remembrance of things that are to come with those that shall come after" (Ecc. 1:8-11).

Life's Brevity
How brief is man's lifespan when seen against the seemingly endless processes of the natural world! A person's time on earth comes to an end so quickly that one wonders if the effort to accomplish anything is really worthwhile. The Preacher seems to be saying: "What does a man really gain from all of his hard work? One generation is quickly replaced by another, but the world about us continues to go on and on," (see Ecc. 1:3-4).

When you look up at the stars, you realize that these are the same luminaries which shone upon Abraham, Isaac, and Jacob. Even trees live hundreds of years. But human beings grow old and die so soon. It seems as if man, in spite of all his mental powers, is of little more importance than the leaves that fall from the trees and are blown away.

When Solomon had such thoughts, he was feeling the prick of the goads of human wisdom. Many people never let themselves think about the brevity of their existence. They push thoughts of death out of their minds, acting as if they will be on earth forever. But a wise person cannot help but do some solemn reflecting as he thinks of the generations who have lived and died while the processes of nature continued on and on. He feels the sharp jab of a goad when he asks himself the question, "Does life have any purpose? Do we continue to exist after we die?" These are painful thoughts, but the wise man will not suppress or sublimate them.

Nature's Aimlessness

The second thought that came to Solomon's mind as he studied creation was the disturbing realization that nature seems to have no purpose or goal. He recounts how the sun rises every morning and sets every evening, how the wind blows south and north and around in a monotonous circle, and how the streams run steadily into the sea without ever filling it (see Ecc. 1:5-7). Nature just does not seem to be heading anywhere. The processes of decomposition and evaporation constantly repeat themselves. The animal population is controlled because they feed upon one another. Great disasters such as earthquakes, hurricanes, and floods destroy years of natural growth, and make a new beginning necessary. What a monotonous cycle! What is life all about in such a world? To this serious question, nature provides no answer. It is therefore a painful thought, and is another goad which can arouse a person from spiritual indifference and send him on a quest for God.

You see, when a man studies the natural world in his own wisdom, he ultimately is confronted by evidence that points in two directions. On the one hand are the signs of order, beauty, and happiness. Such evidence suggests that the world has a powerful, wise, and good Creator. On the other hand, one sees disharmony, cruelty, pain, and death. These things make it appear as if the material world came into existence through a series of accidents.

A sensitive observation of the natural world can point a thinking man to a great Designer and Maker, a Supreme Being. But it cannot tell him that God is love, that He cares for us, and that an eternal destiny awaits every one of us. True, sometimes nature does seem to say that God is good, loving, and kind. A person who is blessed with material benefits, enjoys good health, and faces no immediate danger may walk through an orchard blooming in the springtime or heavy with fruit in the fall and exclaim, "God is good!" Two young lovers on a summer evening, basking in the light of twinkling stars and the golden moon, can easily believe that God is smiling down upon them and that no harm will ever enter their happy world.

But that is only one side of "mother nature." Sometimes she can be brutal. She can kill with the bitter cold of a merciless, swirling blizzard, the fury of a hurricane, or the awesome terror of a devastating earthquake. Thinking about ferocious beasts, poisonous serpents, injurious insects, and disease-producing germs will never lead a person to believe in a loving God.

A person who studies the natural world without

the aid of divine revelation, therefore, will never understand the contradictions he encounters. But if he is willing to acknowledge his inability to resolve these conflicts, he will be goaded into a further quest for light in an attitude of humility. He will then realize that if he is to find stability in life, he must be willing to accept the well-driven nails of God's truth outlined in the Bible.

The Nails of Special Revelation

In the first chapter of Ecclesiastes, the Preacher is content to set forth only goads. Therefore we must turn to other Scripture passages to find the nails of divine truth on the subject of natural revelation. When we do, we will discern two important facts: (1) God has made Himself known in nature, but this self-disclosure is clouded by the results of the fall of Adam; and (2) natural revelation can be fully appreciated and understood only in the light of the Bible.

Real But Clouded

The reality of God's revelation in the natural world is expressed in these words of Paul: "For the invisible things of Him from the creation of the world are clearly seen, being understood by the things that are made, even His eternal power and Godhead, so that they are without excuse" (Rom. 1: 20).

The truth of this declaration is confirmed by human experience. Men who study the universe, even from naturalistic presuppositions, can hardly escape an intuitive conviction that behind it is Someone or something powerful in action and supreme in essence.

The poet David also asserted that God can be

seen in nature. "The heavens declare the glory of God, and the firmament showeth His handiwork. Day unto day uttereth speech, and night unto night showeth knowledge. There is no speech nor language, where their voice is not heard" (Ps. 19:1-3). Yes, the heavens do sing a perpetual anthem to their Maker and express His glory in a language more universal than any human tongue.

But this revelation of God in nature is obscured in two ways: (1) The created world is under the curse because of sin; and (2) man, who proudly tries to interpret its message, is himself blinded by his sinfulness. As a result, he does not understand what he sees. He tries to account for the disharmony in nature without accepting the teaching of the Bible. This leads him down the dead-end streets of frustration and despair. Solomon himself went through this, and that is why he opened the Book of Ecclesiastes by saying, "Vanity of vanities . . . all is vanity" (Ecc. 1:2).

Light of Scripture Needed

Nature's testimony about God can be properly understood only by a person who has accepted in faith the message of the Bible. When the believer gazes into the night sky, admires the beauty of the setting sun, or strolls through an orchard where branches hang heavy with fruit, he is overwhelmed with gratitude for God's great goodness. Even when he hears about earthquakes, tornadoes, and hurricanes, or reflects upon the magnitude of human suffering, he is not perplexed or dismayed. From the Bible the believer knows that these unpleasant aspects of life are the result of sin, and that salvation has been provided through Jesus Christ. His confidence in God's love remains unshaken.

Two men on the Radio Bible Class staff—Henry Bosch and Clair Hess—expressed the Christian's response to the Lord's self-revelation in nature through a song entitled "God's Autograph."*

> I saw God write His autograph upon a moving stream,
> While I, a creature of His hand, sat idly by to dream;
> I saw Him write His powerful name across a stormy sky,
> The pen He used was dipped in fire—I did not question why.
> But when I saw His mighty hand, the plainest on my part,
> Was when He autographed His name with love —across my heart.
> I saw God write His autograph upon the Sacred Page—
> Sweet message of redeeming grace for every race and age;
> Amazed, I saw Him write again upon the cross of shame,
> With pen divine all dipped in blood, "Forgiv'n in Jesus' name!"
> 'Twas then I saw His mighty hand; by faith I did my part,
> And by His grace He wrote His name with love —across my heart.

I can look back with gratitude to my boyhood, for I was taught to observe the natural world from a Christian perspective. My father, Dr. M. R. De Haan, keenly appreciated the beauty all around us. He often spoke about God's handiwork in the universe, and thrilled us as he described the intri-

---

* © 1965 by Singspiration, Inc. Used by permission.

cate movement of the heavenly spheres. His fasci-
nation with the created world led him to maintain
a beautiful garden and keep bees as a hobby. I
vividly recall his explanation of the wonders of
plant life and the marvels of a bee colony. And he
always pointed us to God as the One who is in
ultimate control of everything.

I especially remember an occasion when my
brother and I were frightened during an electrical
storm. My father calmly led us out onto the porch
to watch, while he told us that the lightning is
caused by the meeting of two clouds, one charged
with positive and the other with negative electric-
ity. He explained that the thunder is the sound
caused by the air coming back together after being
split by the flash of fire. But then he pointed out
that God guides the lightning, and that it will not
strike any of His children apart from His will. From
that time on I did not fear a great storm. When I
grew older, the message of Psalm 29 (please read
it!) became clear because of this experience, for I
could hear in the thunder the mighty voice of the
Lord, and see in the lightning flashes a glimpse of
His glory.

In summary, nature's eloquent testimony is properly understood only by the one who knows God
through Jesus Christ. But the non-Christian can
also benefit from nature's witness, for it should
produce within him an intuitive conviction that a
Designer and Maker of the universe exists. If he
responds to this impulse, serious thoughts will come
to him as goads, even as they did to Solomon. He
will think of his weakness and the brevity of his
earthly life, and will be concerned about his relationship to God. When he humbly submits to these
reflections and the questions they raise, he will be

drawn to the Bible. But he will be driven to despair if he proudly tries to provide the answers on his own. If he will admit his need and acknowledge the nails of divine truth, he will be led to exclaim, "Oh, Lord, our Lord, how excellent is Thy name in all the earth!" (Ps. 8:9) If not, he will lament in bitterness, "Vanity of vanities . . . all is vanity" (Ecc. 1:2).

3

Thinkers, Past and Passed

If a nationally known philosopher and theologian were to announce a series of lectures entitled "The Nature of Epistemology and the Absurdity of Metaphysics," he would not draw a very large crowd. Only a scattering of professors, a handful of university students, a preacher or two, and maybe a few pseudo-intellectuals would make up his audience. If Solomon were living in that community, I imagine he would be present. But folks who like deep books and lectures on philosophy are the exception rather than the rule. The mere mention of such themes turns most people off. I am going to assume you do not want to wade through a chapter that belongs in a treatise on philosophy.

I would like to point out, however, that at times all of us think about philosophical or theological subjects. One cannot help but think seriously when he attends the funeral of a loved one. A young couple can hardly bring a new baby home from the hospital without feeling a sense of awe as they talk about the marvel of birth and their new responsibility. It frightens them to realize they have been given a human being with a lifetime potential for good or evil. Down in their hearts they cannot think of their little one as being only a complex mechanism of flesh and bone.

Then, too, almost everyone experiences occasional gnawing feelings of anxiety and terror. Usually these emotions are hard to define or analyze. They include a sense of guilt, a fear of punishment, a horror of the unknown, and a dread of death. These thoughts and feelings give rise to a number of questions: *Who am I? Do I have an immortal soul? Why am I here? How can I know what is right and wrong? What will happen to me after I die?* These are basic problems of existence and men have grappled with them since the beginning of time.

One might think that after thousands of years we would have solved most of these vexing difficulties, but that has not been the case. In fact, our day is marked by a depth of despair concerning these questions unparalleled in history.

Scientists have been able to make great strides in space technology and nuclear research, but the elusive goal of peace in their own hearts continues to escape their grasp. Archaeologists and geologists have made astonishing discoveries, but have not yet been able to come up with a satisfactory explanation of the origin of the world or man. We have spent millions of dollars researching the problems of human behavior, but violent crime continues to increase and mental disorders are more prevalent than ever before. Though it is painful to admit, we must face the fact that our world is filled with misery, fear, doubt, mistrust, and unhappiness of every kind.

The Bankruptcy of Human Wisdom

The failure of man's wisdom is vividly expressed by Solomon in the first chapter of Ecclesiastes. After unsuccessful attempts to find God and spiritual satisfaction in a study of nature and history, he turned to the literature of his day. Again he was frustrated. "I gave my heart to seek and search out by wisdom concerning all things that are done under heaven; this severe travail hath God given to the sons of men to be exercised therewith. I have seen all the works that are done under the sun and, behold, all is vanity and vexation of spirit. For in much wisdom is much grief; and he that increaseth knowledge increaseth sorrow" (Ecc. 1:13-14, 18).

The Preacher says his long hours of study became burdensome (a "severe travail"), but he pressed on in the conviction that his search would lead to satisfactory answers. Yet twice in this brief passage he expresses keen disappointment. The words in verse 14 translated "vexation of spirit" would be more accurately rendered "like chasing the wind." Then Solomon closes this section with despairing words. The more he learned, the more he realized how many questions remained unanswered. As his knowledge increased, so did his feelings of grief and despair.

The realization that human wisdom fails to answer life's basic problems is painful for the man who has never found God as He is revealed in the Scriptures. It is one of the goads Solomon referred to in the closing chapter of Ecclesiastes. You remember that we identified the goads as sharp pricks that come to the mind and conscience when one confronts life realistically and admits that he cannot solve its problems in his own wisdom. Most people do not like to face up to this, but the experience of men throughout history coincides with Solomon's statement that philosophical endeavor is like "chasing the wind."

This Bankruptcy Demonstrated

A survey of philosophical thought from the time of Plato to the present confirms the accuracy of the Preacher's conclusions. Philosophy really has been going in circles. A carefully contrived belief system is set forth by one brilliant thinker, only to be demolished by another man of equal learning. He in turn sets up his own schema, but it is riddled by the bullets of a third man's reasoning powers. This process has repeated itself continually throughout the centuries.

Plato and Aristotle

Greek philosophy reached its zenith in the works of Plato and Aristotle. Yet these two men presented ideas which can never be reconciled.

Plato (427-347 B.C.) said that the world we perceive with our senses is only a shadow, a copy of the true and eternal world of spiritual "forms" or ideas. He declared that one can understand life and discover reality only through philosophical speculation. His concepts implied that scientific investigation of what we can see and touch is unimportant, since the physical world is not real anyway.

Aristotle (384-322 B.C.) took almost the opposite view. He said that only the individual objects we can see and touch are real. Although he insisted that the universe has some kind of unchanging cause, he felt that a spirit world of "forms" does not exist. For example, he said that *goodness* has no reality apart from its manifestation in people who are good.

These opposing views continued in force down through the centuries. By the time Christ came to earth, the thinkers of the day had stopped trying to reconcile them. Most philosophers had become skeptics, taking either the stoical position of simply accepting one's lot with courage, or the epicurean viewpoint that mental or physical pleasure is the only important goal of life.

The Middle Ages

Although medieval times produced some great thinkers like Anselm, Abelard, and Aquinas, most philosophers of that era argued endlessly over the issues raised by Plato and Aristotle. They tried to merge Christian doctrine with human philosophy, but largely neglected the careful study of the Scriptures. Anyone who reads about their hair-splitting theological debates finds little mental or spiritual satisfaction. The obscurity of language and thought is frustrating, and in general the scholars were far more interested in the interpretation of the ancient Greeks than in God's revelation. Christians were poorly instructed and were deprived of the biblical truths that can lead to spiritual peace and joy. The best of man's wisdom again failed to satisfy the deeper longings of the soul.

The Reformation to the Enlightenment

The philosophical methods of man changed as a result of the great revival of art, literature, and learning which took place in Europe during the 14th, 15th, and 16th centuries. Two distinct methods of approach to the problems of existence became popular during that time: rationalism and empiricism. Rationalists maintain that the exercise of reason provides the only valid basis for action or belief, while empiricists say experience, especially of the senses, is the only source of knowledge.

A number of leading philosophers of this age thought they could bring about a union of Christian theology and human philosophy, but it was theology that suffered in the attempt. The trend gradually went from theism (belief in a personal God) to deism (the concept of God as an impersonal force or power). David Hume (1711-1776), gave up this attempt at harmonization, and became a pessimist and skeptic. He epitomized the failure of human wisdom during this period of time. Bertrand Russell, in his *History of Western Philosophy*, said: "Hume's philosophy, whether true or false, represents the bankruptcy of 18th century reasonableness." Every system of thought led men down a blind alley. They began to doubt that any of life's great questions could ever be answered.

The 19th Century

The skepticism that prevailed at the close of the 18th century triggered ferment and turmoil both in theological and philosophical circles. In philosophy a new way of thinking began to make an impact. Up to this time, men had thought that they could arrive at a consistent belief-sytem through proving one idea to be true and its opposite to be false. But the German philosopher Kant, in criticizing man's ultimate faith in pure reason, laid the foundation for a change. Afttr denying that man can prove or disprove the reality of God by rational arguments, he sought to establish God's existence and eternality by the use of "practical reason." He affirmed that one must formulate his beliefs on the basis of what he feels and experiences in his day-by-day encounters with life's problems.

Hegel built upon Kant's concepts, advancing the new system by saying that one can never really arrive at truth. He can only work toward it by the process of setting up a thesis, considering its opposite, and then producing a synthesis out of these contradictory ideas. The new idea then must go through the same process. No ultimate truth can ever be attained in this manner, however, for each conclusion has an antithesis to be considered.

All of this paved the way for Kierkegaard's contention that one must see truth on two levels. The lower platform is the logical position one takes as he studies scientific evidence. The higher level is one of faith in God and the message of the Bible. He said this upper story can be reached only through an "irrational leap." Kierkegaard held to the basic doctrines of the Christian faith, but his idea of a "leap in the dark" does a terrible injustice to our faith in the veracity of the Scriptures. His thinking has been extremely influential upon current existential thought.

The 20th Century

As our century began, religious leaders were in a state of flux. Some theologians who had departed from belief in biblical inspiration were desperately seeking a belief-system that would include Bible truths, yet allow belief in Darwinian evolution. Others, in quest for a way to harmonize human philosophy with orthodox Christian doctrine, were going back to the works of Thomas Aquinas. But none brought stability or peace.

Although the bankruptcy of human wisdom had made an impact upon some philosophers, most people remained optimistic. Scientific advances held great promise, and it was generally felt that men would become better through increased learning. A time of universal peace and prosperity seemed to be just around the corner.

These hopes have been dashed by World War

I, the Great Depression, World War II, and post-war conditions. As a result, the hopelessness of the philosophers—who long since have despaired of finding a unified system of thought—has finally reached down to the man in the street.

Contemporary Thinking

Os Guinness, in his book *The Dust of Death*, points out that three attitudes are prevalent in contemporary thinking: optimism, pessimism, and mechanisms for escaping reality. We will briefly examine each of them.

Irrational Optimism

Many people speak in glowing terms of a golden tomorrow, but close their eyes to the unpleasant realities of life. Though they can find no valid basis for doing so, they continue to have confidence in reason, to trust in progress, to be assured that science is good, and to rely upon man's self-sufficiency. And, all the while they *know* they are refusing to be realistic! They are actually being dishonest with themselves. Kenneth Clark, leading British historian and thinker, correctly criticized them when he wrote, "Confident articles on the future seem to me, intellectually, the most disreputable of all forms of public utterance."

Bleak Pessimism

A second option chosen by some men and women today is that set forth by the pessimists. They see only a bleak future and face life with a desperate courage. They do nothing more than try to make the present as enjoyable as possible. The late Bertrand Russell is an outstanding example of a man who believed the world was doomed to destruction and despair. He championed causes he believed to be humanitarian, but steadfastly refused to enter-

tain a single ray of hope about eternity. Shortly before his death he could only say, "I've had some
good innings."

Escape from Reality

A growing percentage of today's society is select-
ing a third alternative. While they agree with the
pessimist's view that the world is without purpose
or meaning, they seek an escape from its consequences, often through an emotionally charged experience. These people try to break away from the
despair of life by turning to hallucinatory drugs,
the pantheistic Eastern religions, the occult, gross
sensualism, or other escapes. Another pathway, followed by an intellectual few, is existentialism. This
allows a person to take an "irrational leap of faith,"
by which he blindly accepts something he won't
even attempt to defend or understand. He may
even try to "authenticate" his existence through
some kind of extreme act which creates a powerful
feeling.

Most people who are not Christians and do not
believe in the Bible choose to live either in a fan-
tasy world of unfounded optimism or turn to one
of the irrational escapes enumerated above. Obviously, the philosophies of man have not succeeded
in meeting the basic needs of mankind. They have
all proved to be dead-end streets.

God's Wisdom Meets Man's Need

Human experience has amply demonstrated the
bankruptcy of man's wisdom. Honest people everywhere have recognized their need for an authori-
tative message originating outside of themselves
or the world. Solomon said exactly this in the closing chapter of Ecclesiastes, pointing men to the
"nails . . . that come from one shepherd." This

"one Shepherd" is God, and the "nails" are the truths which come to us from His Word, the Bible.

The Apostle Paul, living at a time when the shortcomings of Grecian philosophy had become apparent, presented a most striking contrast between man's wisdom and that which comes from God. It is recorded in the first and second chapters of 1 Corinthians.

In this passage Paul affirms that the message of a crucified Saviour, which men termed "foolishness," had in turn "made foolish" the clever arguments of the philosophers and religionists of that day. "For the preaching of the cross is to them that perish foolishness; but unto us who are saved it is the power of God. For it is written, I will destroy the wisdom of the wise, and will bring to nothing the understanding of the prudent. Where is the wise? Where is the scribe? Where is the disputer of this age? Hath not God made foolish the wisdom of this world? For after that, in the wisdom of God, the world by wisdom knew not God, it pleased God by the foolishness of preaching to save them that believe. For the Jews require a sign, and the Greeks seek after wisdom; but we preach Christ crucified, unto the Jews a stumbling block, and unto the Gentiles foolishness" (1 Cor. 1:18-23).

In Paul's day, as in ours, the wisdom of men had degenerated into futility and produced a corrupt society. But the message of the cross, God's wisdom to men, brought salvation to all who believed. Followers of Christ often came from the ranks of the uneducated and poor (see 1 Cor. 1:26-29). Yet, they lived in confidence and joy, and exerted a tremendous influence upon their culture. Through their union with Jesus Christ they were given true wisdom (see 1 Cor. 1:30). This brought them a new standing before God, a new inner power for holiness, and a new freedom from the effects of sin.

This wisdom of God came to earth through Jesus Christ, the incarnate Word, and is revealed in the written Word, the Bible. It is so distinctive in its supernatural origin and power that the Christian evangelist or preacher presents this truth in direct contrast to the methods of the philosopher or historian. Paul did not have to use distracting oratorical tricks, subtle philosophical suggestions, or theological double-talk to persuade men. He could speak clearly and authoritatively. Because he knew he would be ineffective in his own strength, he just preached the Gospel. Energized by the Holy Spirit, it had great power to reach the hearts of men.

"And I, brethren, when I came to you, came not with excellency of speech or of wisdom, declaring unto you the testimony of God. For I determined not to know anything among you, except Jesus Christ, and Him crucified. And I was with you in weakness, and in fear, and in much trembling. And my speech and my preaching were not with enticing words of man's wisdom, but in demonstration of the Spirit and of power; that your faith should not stand in the wisdom of men, but in the power of God" (1 Cor. 2:1-5).

Paul was a highly educated and widely read man, and could easily have embellished his preaching with numerous references to the works of famous scholars. But he deliberately avoided this temptation. He knew that if people accepted Christianity on the basis of a moving speech or a series of clever arguments, they might be mere professors of faith without experiencing God's transforming power.

When he arrived at Corinth, he was overwhelmed

with the gigantic task of preaching the Gospel to this thoroughly heathen city. He knew that the successful proclamation of God's truth does not require the delivery of beautifully worked out sermons, but could be found in the straightforward declaration of salvation through faith in the Lord Jesus Christ.

In summary, the goad of Ecclesiastes 1:12-18 is the disturbing realization that man's wisdom is incomplete and misleading. It has always failed. But, thank God, we need not depend upon our own meager philosophical systems. God has spoken in His Son, and we have in His Word a reliable record of His provision for our salvation. Whenever a person acknowledges his sinfulness, admits his inability to save himself by good works, and places his faith in Jesus Christ, he is delivered from the penalty and power of sin. He experiences spiritual transformation and enters into a joy he never thought possible. How much better to trust Christ than continue walking the dead-end streets of human wisdom!

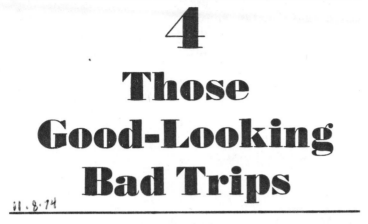

4

Those Good-Looking Bad Trips

11.8.74

The newspapers recently carried a story about a pathetic shopkeeper who sells used books and periodicals. He graduated from an elite university, was a playboy for a few years, dabbled in drugs and the activities of the New Left, and then achieved success both in business and in a distinguished profession. But now, not yet 50 years of age, he looks upon all of his past pleasures and accomplishments as totally futile. Nothing has any real significance to him. Why? Because he does not believe in God and life after death.

This man's experiences led him to two conclusions: that unrestrained sensualism produces more pain than pleasure, and that hard work is sheer foolishness. That is why he decided to operate a business that requires little effort and makes few demands upon him. He is unkempt in appearance and thinks of his life as a meaningless interlude in a process which will eventually lead to his extinction. He has become another victim of the unbelief so prevalent in our contemporary world.

In the quest for happiness and satisfaction, many people have tried religions and philosophies, while others have experimented with mysticism, occult practices and hallucinatory drugs. Still others have openly declared pleasure to be the goal of their lives. Each individual seeks pleasure in his own way. Gross sensualism, financial success, fame, and cultural pursuits are among the avenues people have walked in their efforts to find happiness through pleasure. And many have spared no effort to achieve their goals.

Paths of Pleasure

The pleasure-seeking pattern of modern man corresponds precisely to Solomon's experience. In Ecclesiastes 2 he tells us that after he could not find spiritual peace or meaning for life through the use of his reasoning powers, he first tried sensualism, then great human achievement, and finally the refined pleasure of the arts.

Revelry

The Preacher began his new quest for happiness by plunging into a life of frivolous gaiety. Here is his description: "I said in mine heart, Come now, I will test thee with mirth. . . . What doeth it?" (Ecc. 2:1-2)

Solomon soon found that a continuous round of revelry brought only short-term dividends. In a later passage he concluded that laughter is like the crackling of burning thorns (see Ecc. 7:6). They blaze forth with great promise but last only a moment, giving off little heat and leaving nothing more substantial than a few cold, gray ashes. His brief pleasures were more than offset by the inevitable gloom that followed when he was alone with his thoughts.

Wine

Solomon also experimented with strong drink in his attempt to find pleasure. "I sought in mine heart to give myself unto wine, yet acquainting mine heart with wisdom, and to lay hold on folly, till I might see what was that good for the sons of men, which they should do under the heaven all the days of their life" (Ecc. 2:3).

Apparently Solomon thought that under the influence of wine he might obtain deeper insights than those which come through sober reflection, but again he was disappointed. The stimulation afforded by alcohol did not give him the flashes of awareness he was seeking. He did not let himself become a slave of drink during this time, however, for he used his intelligence to avoid the trap of making alcohol a crutch, an opiate, or an escape. So when he realized it offered him no help, he abandoned it.

Culture and Refinement

The king of Israel next turned to a life of achievement, culture, and refined pleasure in a search for happiness. The lengths to which he went are described in the following passage: "I made for myself great works; I built houses; I planted vineyards; I made gardens and orchards, and I planted trees in them of all kind of fruits; I made pools of water, to water therewith the wood that bringeth forth trees. I got servants and maidens, and had servants born in my house; also I had great possessions of herds and flocks above all that were in Jerusalem before me. I gathered also silver and gold, and the peculiar treasure of kings and of the provinces; I got men singers and women singers, and the delights of the sons of men, as musical instruments, and that of all sorts.

"So I was great, and increased more than all that were before me in Jerusalem; also my wisdom remained with me. And whatsoever mine eyes desired, I kept not from them. I withheld not my heart from any joy; for my heart rejoiced in all my labor; and this was my portion of all my labor. Then I looked on all the works that my hands had wrought, and on the labor that I had labored to do; and, behold, all was vanity and vexation of spirit, and there was no profit under the sun" (Ecc. 2:4-11).

Solomon's palaces were splendid. His vineyards were large and well cultivated. His parks and gardens were beautifully designed and maintained. His plantations were abundantly watered from man-made reservoirs. His household staff, his vast wealth, his command-performance entertainers were of fabled reputation. Solomon filled his life with every conceivable delight. Yet all the while he conducted himself in a manner which earned him the respect and admiration of his peers, for he declares, "My wisdom remained with me."

It appears that for a short time Solomon found gratification in this life of magnificence and luxury. His mind was kept occupied and his senses were pleasurably excited. His ego was bolstered when men praised him for his wealth and accomplishments. But alas, these good feelings did not endure. The thrill gradually wore off. He took a second look at all he had achieved, the wealth he had amassed, and the sensations he had enjoyed. And when he did, he was overwhelmed with a feeling of deep despair. He saw that everything he had been doing was futile, empty, and unprofitable.

The goads of serious thinking had driven him into this state of despair. Even while he was filling his life with the pleasures just described, a sequence of reflections kept returning to his mind, and he could not get away from them. Though he was the most wealthy and talented king in his day, and could experiment with everything this world affords, his troubled mind kept him from enjoying life fully.

The Emptiness of Pleasure

One of the problems Solomon faced all through his time of experimentation was the growing awareness that the enjoyment of physical pleasure does not last very long. When he seriously considered his future happiness, it was impossible for him to live only for the satisfaction of his physical desires. That is why he eventually turned from revelry and wine to cultural pursuits.

Here is the Preacher's description of how he felt. "And I turned myself to behold wisdom, and madness, and folly; for what can the man do that cometh after the king? Even that which hath been already done. Then I saw that wisdom excelleth folly, as far as light excelleth darkness. The wise man's eyes are in his head, but the fool walketh in darkness" (Ecc. 2:12-14).

Solomon came to the conclusion that a life given over to pleasure is "folly." And the experience of man confirms this observation. The Roman civilization began with high moral standards, an emphasis upon the sanctity of the home, and a passion for honesty and justice. But because of the decline of the culture and an extravagant prosperity, the people began to live immorally, the home broke down, and even the courts became corrupted. As a result, society gradually decayed, and the barbarians from the north were able to overrun the land.

This same process takes place in the lives of individuals as well as in society. A person who thinks in terms of "me only," ignoring the fact that his actions deeply affect other people, finds no genuine personal satisfaction and becomes a degrading influence in the lives of others.

This is vividly illustrated in our own day. Determined voices crying out against a puritanical attitude toward sexual freedom have prevailed enough to bring about drastic changes. But the result of this new freedom has not been as wonderful as anticipated. Men and women are learning that they cannot live happily without love and the feeling that they are needed and wanted. They are discovering these needs to be far more important than the biological and physical aspects of sex. The selfish, detached sensualism so strenuously advocated in many quarters, as exemplified in the "playboy" philosophy, has turned out to be a curse in today's society.

It does not take a great deal of wisdom to conclude that one should seek lasting happiness rather than that which will give only a momentary thrill. A sensible person will realize that he should look for happiness on a long-range basis.

Death Is Inevitable

The second goad in Solomon's thinking was his realization that death is both inevitable and impartial. If he could only have kept himself from thinking about eternity, he could have found a great deal more satisfaction in his cultural achievements and worthwhile attainments. But he could not! The awareness that life is but a moment compared to eternity, and that nothing earthly can satisfy, forced itself upon him at the least expected times.

Undoubtedly thoughts of death became more persistent with the passing years. Even when he abandoned the pursuit of happiness through gross forms of sensualism, he was still pursued by the knowledge that death comes to all men alike. "I myself perceived also that one event happeneth to them all. Then said I in my heart, 'As it happeneth to the fool, so it happeneth even to me; and why was I then more wise?' Then I said in my heart, that this also is vanity. For there is no remembrance of the wise more than of the fool forever, seeing that which now is in the days to come shall all be forgotten. And how dieth the wise man? Like the fool. Therefore I hated life, because the work that is wrought under the sun is grievous unto me; for all is vanity and vexation of spirit" (Ecc. 2:14-17).

When a person without faith in God concludes that all men come to the same dismal end, he can easily decide that nothing is worthwhile. He then envies the dropouts of society who seem to sidestep or sublimate all thoughts about the future and live without responsibility. It may appear that these are the most successful of all men.

Ideas like these haunt the minds of many people today, and we should not think this strange. After all, if a person has no faith in God, he has little reason to reckon with the reality of anything beyond this life. No wonder many talk about human existence as a bad accident, look upon every human achievement as a worthless bauble, and consider death to be a frightful leap into the dark unknown! Such thinking drives people to drink, drugs, occult practices, or various kinds of irrational philosophy. On the other hand, it leads some to a real and meaningful faith in Christ.

Men sometimes make beautiful statements about

death: it is "as natural as being born" / "a joining of the majority" / "an ending of all unfair and painful distinctions among men" / "a leaving to go to a better world." Unless these declarations are based upon something more than a mere wish, they have no value. It is frightening to face death without faith in God.

What About Your Successor?

The third goad that disturbed Solomon was his realization that a person has no control over what happens to his possessions and the fruit of his labor after he dies. "Yea, I hated all my labor which I had taken under the sun, because I should leave it unto the man that shall be after me. And who knoweth whether he shall be a wise man or a fool? Yet shall he have rule over all my labor wherein I have labored, and wherein I have shown myself wise under the sun. This is also vanity" (Ecc. 2:18-19).

The Preacher declared that a man might toil unceasingly and live respectably only to have his successor be a scoundrel and squander everything. An industrious person could build an empire and make for himself a great name, but have his heir manage things poorly and let everything crumble in ruins. A prudent man is not assured that even his good name or beneficial achievements will endure after he dies. These thoughts, coupled with the fact that all men must die and go to the grave, will eat away at the happiness of any man who tries to find satisfaction in life apart from God.

Having reported that his logical thinking processes had deeply disturbed him, so that he could not find satisfaction in sensualism, culture, or achievement, Solomon proceeds to give us the wisdom which comes from above. Remember, he had been taught the truths of the Old Testament Scriptures, and he could not escape the basic principles about right and wrong he had learned in his childhood. He presents us with two nails of revealed truth in Ecclesiastes 2:24-26.

Faith Brings Contentment

Solomon declares that a man who believes in the God revealed in the Scriptures will find satisfaction in simple activities like eating, drinking, and working. This is what he says in Ecclesiastes 2:24-25. A number of leading Hebrew scholars, including Delitzsch, Plumptre, and M'Neile, interpret these verses to mean: "There is nothing better for a man than to eat and drink and cause a soul to see good in his labor. For even this, I saw, comes from the hand of God; for who can eat and enjoy himself apart from Him?"

The man who recognizes that all he is and all he has comes from the hand of God can partake of the most simple fare with a grateful heart. He can look upon his labor, however menial, as having significance. While Solomon with all of his wealth and learning could not find contentment through human scholarship, sensual living, great achievements, or cultural activities, an ordinary slave who knew the Lord could sit down with his family and take delight in a simple meal. He could eat and drink in gratitude, for he saw his provisions as coming from God's hands. This man could find a sense of fulfillment even though he spent the day hoeing weeds, carrying mortar, or cleaning a stable, for he performed his work as one who has been assigned the task by God himself.

This nail of divine truth is confirmed throughout

the Old Testament. The creation story tells us man was made in the image and likeness of God, and designed for fellowship with his Maker. The Psalms repeatedly define the happy man as one who finds great pleasure in "the law of the Lord" (Ps. 1:2). They teach that a poor man who knows and worships God is far more wealthy than the rich man who tries to live as if God did not exist.

The New Testament also encourages us to include God in every detail of our day-by-day existence. Human reason would lead a person to believe that the Almighty cannot be bothered with us and our petty little problems. But our Saviour taught us to pray, "Give us this day our daily bread" (Matt. 6:11), showing us that God is interested and involved in our basic physical requirements.

The Apostle Paul confirmed Solomon's declaration that we may find pleasure in a simple meal because both the food itself and our capacity to enjoy it are gifts from God. He told Christians who were being misled by legalists who advocated stringent dietary regulations that every edible product in God's creation has been given for man's benefit. (see 1 Tim. 4:4-5).

A man of faith can also see that his secular labor is good. Paul pointed out that a Christian is to view his vocation as a part of God's will for him. "Servants, obey in all things your masters according to the flesh; not with eyeservice, as menpleasers, but in singleness of heart, fearing God. And whatever ye do, do it heartily, as to the Lord, and not unto men, knowing that of the Lord ye shall receive the reward of the inheritance; for ye serve the Lord Christ" (Col. 3:22-24).

The Christian slave was to be diligent in his

work, for faithful service to his master would bring honor to the Lord Jesus Christ. Other men might work hard only when under the eye of a foreman, but the believer should always be conscientious, realizing that he is actually serving Christ. His motive for diligence is not to be the fear of his boss, but respect and love for the Lord. Even if his human supervisors do not reward him properly, he is not to be discouraged. He knows that the Lord Jesus, the Saviour to whom he belongs and whom he serves, will take care of the matter righteously.

When a child of God evaluates his labor as being good in the Lord's sight, his work takes on new meaning. Thousands, working at jobs which give little satisfaction, carry on mechanically day after day only for the sake of the paycheck. But when one truly knows Christ and gives a day's work for a day's pay, he can look upon his tasks as service "unto the Lord."

After all, God made this earth and the people who live in it, and each of us fills a little place in His total program. When we do our jobs well and manifest a cheerful and Christlike attitude, we bring glory to the Lord Jesus. The commonplace becomes rich and meaningful. The nonbeliever may become frustrated in the performance of his duties, even if he has a place of great responsibility and earthly reward. The Christian, on the other hand, will find satisfaction no matter where the Lord has placed him or what He calls upon him to do.

Faith Brings Wisdom and Joy
The second nail of divine revelation is found at the close of Ecclesiastes 2. "For God giveth to a man that is good in His sight wisdom, and knowledge, and joy; but to the sinner He giveth travail, to

gather and to heap up, that he may give to him that is good before God. This also is vanity and vexation of spirit" (Ecc. 2:26).

The Lord bestows "wisdom and knowledge" upon those who trust Him, and therefore an uneducated believer can have a far better comprehension of what life is all about than a brilliant scientist who rejects the Word of God. As mentioned in an earlier chapter, he knows why nature contains both beauty and ugliness, pain and pleasure, growth and destruction. He may not grasp all the facts of history, but he knows God is at work in it and looks forward with assurance to the new heavens and new earth of which the Scriptures speak.

God also gives "joy" to those who are "good in His sight." The believer is happy in his life of submission to the Lord. People around him may think he is depriving himself of many pleasures because he refuses to do what they do. They may even congratulate themselves, thinking they are having more fun than he is. Yet all the time they have to live with a vague inner feeling that they are missing out on life's best. If they would observe the believer carefully, they would detect a deep joy in his life which they do not have. Sensualism, human achievement, fame, and even the highest form of cultural pleasure cannot produce a fraction of the true happiness experienced by the believer who walks with God.

5

The Heavy Foot of Fate

The father of a girl who had been raped and brutally murdered was interviewed by a newsman for a midwestern TV station. When asked to state his feelings about the tragic event, the grief-stricken parent replied that he accepted it as the permissive will of God, and that He would bring good out of it. The man expressed confidence that his daughter is now in heaven and is supremely happy. In response to a question about the murderer, he declared that he had no desire for revenge. He was glad the man had been apprehended, and was thankful that he would be punished for his deed. Yet he showed a surprising sense of sympathy for the criminal, declaring that only God knows what drives a man to perform such a horrible act. He went on to say that he and his wife were praying that the rapist-murderer would confess his sinfulness and believe on Jesus Christ.

This incident and the resulting interview raise a number of vital questions: (1) Why would God allow a beautiful girl to suffer such a horrible death? (2) Why didn't He step in and prevent this crime? (3) Just how free are people? (4) Is the criminal responsible for his antisocial behavior? (5) Could we have blamed the father of this girl if he had felt like killing the guilty man?

Many of today's psychologists and sociologists, when confronted with questions like this, insist that every event is caused by the blind movements of fate. To them the world and human life are nothing more than the consequences of a series of bad accidents. The existence of a personal God exercising providential control over the world is ruled out. Physical determinists, for example, say that all human conduct is directed by chemical factors involving the brain and glands. To support their position, they point out that the use of hallucinatory drugs or alcohol can radically change a person's actions. They also cite instances when brain injury or a tumor has resulted in aberrant behavior. In addition, many psychiatrists report that massive doses of certain vitamins and minerals are responsible for amazing cures in some neurotic and psychotic people.

But not all specialists believe that human behavior is totally controlled by physical factors. They maintain that the root causes lie deep within the human personality. They admit that biological elements sometimes play a part, but insist that even chemical changes can be psychologically induced.

We do not accept either of these extreme positions, though there may be some validity in each. At their basic level, both groups teach that man is nothing more than a machine. If this presupposition is true, then no one should ever be blamed or punished for wrongdoing, for ultimately he could not control his behavior. By the same token, people who are helpful, kind, and generous should not be praised or rewarded. After all, they too are doing nothing more than acting out inevitable responses to physical or psychological stimuli. No, we strongly disagree with both of these contentions!

The problem of the mysterious ways of God's providence, including the question of human freedom and God's inflexible decrees, has puzzled thinking people through the ages. Certain factors forced upon an individual obviously have an influence upon what he does. On the other hand, society just could not function if everyone denied human responsibility. Solomon discussed the relationship between man's freedom and God's providence in Ecclesiastes 3:1-15.

The Preacher begins by setting forth two conclusions he reached through observation and reflections: (1) man cannot control the events and circumstances of his life; and (2) his efforts to improve his lot are therefore superfluous. These conclusions are goads because they arouse us like a sharp-pointed instrument spurs an ox. Surely the animal can get along without the goad, which does not feel very good. But it accomplishes a significant purpose, for the ox keeps moving. Similarly, the above conclusions are disturbing. But we can hope that they will move people toward Jesus Christ. When a person becomes plagued with guilt, or his system of thought brings him to the brink of despair, the likelihood of his becoming a Christian is greatly increased.

Sometimes You Don't Choose

Solomon says, "To everything there is a season, and a time to every purpose under the heaven" (Ecc. 3:1). People are often unable to determine the direction of their lives. The most carefully charted course may have to be abandoned if sickness, economic upheaval, or death occur. A number of life situations are cited to confirm this truth and show that many events take place outside man's control.

"A time to be born, and a time to die" (Ecc. 3: 2). The instant of a person's birth and the moment of his death are ordered by a power or force outside of himself. Perhaps all of us have thought about the fact that we are living in the 20th century, and have wondered what it would be like if we had been born into some other era. But we could not choose when we would come into the world, and we are unable to set the date of our death, apart from suicide. The vast majority of mankind is helpless before the steady footsteps of the grim reaper. We are facing the problems and joys of today's world because of what some people call the "accident" of birth, and we have no idea when or how we will be snatched away.

"A time to plant, and a time to pluck up that which is planted" (Ecc. 3:2). The farmer or gardener is not wholly free. The climate, the nature of the soil, and seasonal factors limit his selection of crops. He must sow in the springtime and reap in the fall, and no amount of effort on his part can alter these dictums of nature.

"A time to kill, and a time to heal" (Ecc. 3:3). The policeman or soldier in the line of duty must sometimes kill, even though he does not want to. On the other hand, doctors and nurses will work night and day to keep the most desperate criminal alive—even though he was shot a few hours before by a law officer.

"A time to break down, and a time to build up" (Ecc. 3:3). A building is usually razed when its

appearance deteriorates or it becomes unsafe because of age. Sometimes even a relatively new
structure must be torn down in the interests of
progress. Though a certain amount of human freedom is involved in the process, elements over which
we have no control often play the major part in our
decisions.

"*A time to weep, and a time to laugh; a time to
mourn, and a time to dance*" (Ecc. 3:4). The ap-
propriateness of laughter or tears is determined by
circumstances beyond us. While we may weep at
every funeral we attend, we are especially in sorrow when a young person dies. But we laugh happily and enjoy the festivity of a wedding or an
anniversary celebration.

"*A time to cast away stones, and a time to gather
stones together*" (Ecc. 3:5). In these words the
Preacher is probably talking about the important
part stones played during his era. On some days
the farmer picked up stones and removed them
from his field, but at other times he gathered them
together to construct a fence or building. Again,
circumstances and the pressing need of the moment
dictated which was to be done.

"*A time to embrace, and a time to refrain from
embracing*" (Ecc. 3:5). The mores of society, our
personal emotional responses, and our current situations dictate when we may demonstrate friendship
and love, and when we must not.

"*A time to get, and a time to lose; a time to keep,
and a time to cast away*" (Ecc. 3:6). We do not
have the control that we would like to think we
have over our accumulation of earthly treasure or
its loss. The skills we were born with, the economic
situation of our day, and the opportunities before
us are all contributing forces with which we must

reckon. They often leave us with only one sensible course of action. A sailor in a storm, for example, may decide to throw cargo overboard to lighten the ship, thinking he is doing so as a matter of free choice. Actually, however, he is preserving his life, and he has no option if he wants to survive.

"A *time to tear, and a time to sew*" (Ecc. 3:7). In Solomon's day, one would rip his clothing as an expression of grief; or, if a garment were no longer serviceable, it would be torn into strips for another use. A woman would sew when her family needed clothing, or when mending was required. But no one could control when these times would occur.

"A *time to keep silence, and a time to speak*" (Ecc. 3:7). We have all encountered circumstances, as at formal functions or in potentially embarrassing situations, in which we knew it was best to keep quiet. On other occasions, however, we have felt it absolutely mandatory to say what we think. Again, being silent or speaking out is not fully a matter of free choice.

"A *time to love, and a time to hate; a time of war, and a time of peace*" (Ecc. 3:8). When an enemy power invades our shores determined to destroy our nation and deprive us of our religious freedom, we must hate everything that force represents. We must go to war, not because we like to, but to meet the attack. The time for peace will come later.

Solomon included this long list of life situations to demonstrate that man's range of choice is circumscribed by external conditions. Man seems to be more a victim of circumstances than the master of his own destiny.

All Effort Is Superfluous

The Preacher's observation that man is not really

free is a disturbing thought, and it leads to distressing statements like this: "Well, if what will be will be regardless of anything I do, why should I try to do anything?" This is the basic meaning of Solomon's next statement. "What profit hath he that worketh in that wherein he laboreth? I have seen the travail, which God hath given to the sons of men to be exercised in it" (Ecc. 3:9-10).

If what Solomon said thus far were wholly true, then man is ever victimized by some unknown, unconcerned fate. Why should a person laboriously seek worthwhile goals? After all, whether his endeavors will succeed or fail is determined by laws or accidental occurrences outside his control. If this is how everything works, it is futile to expend mental and physical energy in any direction. Why not just sit back and let the world go by?

Man's Limitations

Although he is the image-bearer of God and conscious of his relation to eternity, man finds himself unable to answer many of life's problems. This is disturbing because we are rational creatures who like to know why we are called upon to pass through trying experiences. We long for explanations of the baffling elements in our existence. The Preacher therefore says, "He hath set the world in their heart, *so that no man can find out the work that God maketh* from the beginning to the end" (Ecc. 3:11).

The meaning of this verse is not clear in the King James translation just given. It would be better read: "He [God] hath set eternity in their [men's] heart, but without giving man the ability to comprehend God's work from beginning to end." Human beings, from their place *under the sun,* can see only the tangled threads on the back of the beautiful tapestry God is weaving. Our limitations as creatures—sinful and fallen creatures at that—prevent our complete understanding of God's providential workings.

But Solomon does not stop there. True, the man without God may well feel that he has no control over his affairs, and that all activity is therefore superfluous. But the Preacher goes on to say that we can avoid giving in to these feelings by appropriating the truths of the Scriptures.

Sober contemplation upon the vicissitudes of life is good exercise if a person is willing to follow through to logical conclusions. He will see that life becomes absurd to the one who does not have faith in the personal God of the Scriptures. This thought process acts as a goad and is painful. But this is exactly the state of mind which prepares one to receive the message of God through the Bible. Solomon, who had experienced all of this himself, provides us with nails of divine revelation on the subject. They teach us how to live happily in a world in which man often appears to be a pawn of fate rather than a free moral agent.

God Has a Perfect Plan

A conscientious study of the Bible reveals that God is unfolding a plan into which every circumstance fits to produce a harmonious, pleasing life under proper conditions. "He hath made everything beautiful in its time" (Ecc. 3:11). This statement is true when we consider it from a Christian perspective, both in its cosmic and personal applications. Each stage of life from childhood to old age has its attractions. Rather than limiting and troubling us, the laws governing the cyclical nature of our world actually add variety, challenge, and value to life under the sun. Even pain, the process of deterioration, sorrow and disappointment play a part in enriching the experience of the one who knows the Lord.

An aged believer, though feeble in body, was still keen mentally. Those who visited him in the rest home always left with a blessing. The aged saint would sometimes talk of his boyhood, his eyes twinkling with merriment as he relived his youthful experiences. With wavering voice he would recount the marvelous ways the Lord had provided during the lean years of the early '30s when his family was growing up. His eyes would glisten with tears as he told how God had wonderfully strengthened him through his wife's illness and death. He saw his youth, adulthood, and now the evening years of life as part of a beautiful process which would lead him to a glorious eternity.

Yes, the biblical truth that "everything is beautiful in its time" can be realized by every child of God. Young people who know the Lord Jesus can be glad for their youth and eagerly anticipate the years of service for Christ which lie ahead of them. Middle-aged believers can be grateful for the earlier stages of life and vigorous in God's service. And many elderly Christians confined to wheelchairs or hospital beds will testify that "all things work together for good to them who love God, to them who are the called according to His purpose" (Rom. 8:28).

This surety about life can be experienced, however, only by those who know the Lord Jesus and walk in fellowship with Him. The man without faith has no such assurance and must view life as the epitome of futility. H. G. Wells, the English novelist, historian, and sociologist, made this statement near the close of his life: "The experiment will be ended, and each one of us will be dissolved into nothingness, like crystals down a drainpipe." How wonderful to be a Christian, and to exclaim triumphantly with Solomon, "Everything is beautiful in its time!"

Man's Sense of Eternity

The second nail is the affirmation that man was made with an intuitive longing for an existence beyond the grave. Alternating between fear and hope, he feels that death does not end all. "He hath set the world [eternity] in their heart, so that no man can find out the work that God maketh from the beginning to the end" (Ecc. 3:11).

The Hebrew word rendered *world* in the King James Version should be translated "forever" or "eternity" in this verse as it is in verse 14 and elsewhere in the Book of Ecclesiastes.

In his physical structure, his bodily functions, and his susceptibility to disease and death, man resembles the animal. But he is distinctive in that he thinks about eternity while the animal does not.

Every normal human being sometimes feels a knot in his stomach as he reflects upon the ultimate future. He finds himself on the horns of a dilemma. He dreads the thought of complete extinction, for built deep within him is a powerful love for life. But he also has guilt feelings, and is afraid he will be punished if he must meet a holy God.

He hardly knows what to believe, and often tries to forget about death and eternity. But no matter how thoroughly he submerges himself in his work, hobbies, or pleasures, he is haunted by the nagging realization that someday he must die. Though he does not like the moral demands of faith in a personal God, he cannot live with the idea that everything is doomed to complete annihilation.

Walt Whitman, envying the carefree existence of the animals, said in *Song of Myself,* "They are so placid and self-contained. They do not lie awake in the dark and weep for their sins; they do not make me sick discussing their duties to God. Not one is dissatisfied . . . not one is respectable or unhappy over the whole earth."

These words of Whitman may strike a responsive chord when one first reads them. One may indeed envy the animals in this respect, but even wishful thinging cannot enable one to fully accept the idea that he *is* only an animal. Try as he may, no normal human being can always, under all circumstances, avoid solemn thoughts about his sins and eternity. Why? Because God "hath set eternity in their heart."

Live Joyously and Obediently

One might expect the well-educated and gifted author of Ecclesiastes to deliver a series of profound statements about the hidden purposes of God, enabling us to face life's mysteries with more understanding. He does not. Instead, he offers these practical words of advice and admonition: "I know that there is no good in them [the affirmations about God's perfect plan, our human consciousness of the eternal, and our limitations], but for a man to rejoice, and to do good in his life; and, also, that every man should eat and drink, and enjoy the good of all his labor, is the gift of God" (Ecc. 3:12-13).

Solomon seems to be saying, "We cannot solve all the mysteries of life. Neither can we ever understand where our control of life ends and God's sovereignty begins. Therefore, I know of nothing better than for us to live joyously and to do what is right, realizing that all life's benefits are gifts from God."

Instead of trying to "unscrew the inscrutable," we should believe and obey that which we can understand. When bewildered by life, our natural tendency is to cry out, "*Why?*" But that does not please the Lord! He wants us to ask, "Father, *what* can I learn from this experience? *What* must I do?" If we trust Him, we will not feel that we need to have all our "whys" answered. We will possess deep serenity even though we do not understand all that happens to us. The important consideration in the life of a person who loves the Lord is to do what is right and to please Him.

On two occasions the Lord Jesus deliberately refused to answer questions of the Apostle Peter, and we can learn from these examples.

The first time was in the Upper Room. When the Saviour came to Peter with a basin and towel to wash his feet, the impulsive disciple asked, "Lord, dost *Thou* wash *my* feet?" It was an expression of bewilderment and a request for an explanation of such condescension.

The Lord simply answered, "What I do thou knowest not now, but thou shalt know hereafter" (John 13:7). At this moment Peter was to allow his feet to be washed by his Master, and it was not necessary for him to understand why.

The second occasion was after our Lord's resurrection. Peter had been restored to fellowship, and Jesus had told him he would someday be taken against his will to prison and death. The unpredictable fisherman then looked toward John and asked what would happen to him. In essence, the Lord Jesus replied, "If it should be My will that he live until I return, what is it to you? You just follow Me" (see John 21:18-22).

We do not need to know the answer to every question. All we need to do is trust God, gratefully accept His blessings, and obey Him.

Fear God

God hides some things from us because He wants us to stand in awe of Him. Solomon said, "I know that, whatsoever God doeth, it shall be forever; nothing can be put to it, nor any thing taken from it; *and God doeth it, that men should fear before Him.* That which hath been is now, and that which is to be hath already been; and God requireth that which is past" (Ecc. 3:14-15).

We are told to fear God, but this thought immediately stimulates several questions. Why should I be afraid of God? Isn't this an Old Testament idea? Doesn't the mention of fear contradict our concept of Him as our loving heavenly Father?

The fear of God mentioned here is not the same as being "scared to death" of the Almighty. It is rather the feeling of awe and reverence in response to God's greatness and glory. It may be compared to the emotions of a person sensitive to creation's majesty as he stands at the foot of a mountain which towers over him, or as he walks gingerly to the edge of the Grand Canyon and looks into its magnificent depths. How small and insignificant he feels at such a moment! Similarly, we as believers in Christ should be overwhelmed when we reflect upon God's greatness and wisdom.

Think of it! Every event of life is part of a perfect, prearranged plan designed for His glory and our good. He is sovereign; yet we operate as free and responsible moral agents. What right have we to question God as if He owed us an explanation for what He does?

Summary

Solomon does not tell us how we can fully harmonize the age-old problem of the relationship between man's freedom and God's sovereignty. Nor does he give us a complete answer to our questions about His ways. Our humanity limits us to such an extent that all our efforts to resolve these baffling mysteries will lead us down dead-end streets. But the Preacher, through inspiration, does give us practical guidelines by which we can live joyously and hopefully in this present world. He says that we must not try to solve theological problems that are beyond us. We are to accept God's blessings with a happy and grateful heart and live before Him in reverence and love.

We who live on this side of Calvary and the empty tomb have far more reason than Solomon to be joyous and triumphant in the face of the mysteries of providence. We can rejoice in the certainty of the salvation already purchased for us, for Jesus *has* come and His work *is* completed.

When the Apostle Paul reflected upon the wonder of what God has done for us in Christ, he broke out in this shout of triumph:
"What shall we then say to these things? If God be for us, who can be against us? He that spared not His own Son, but delivered Him up for us all, how shall He not with Him also freely give us all things?" (Rom. 8:31-32)

God is on our side! He who designed, created, sustains, and rules the universe loves us! This is all we need. We do not even have to walk the dead-end streets of futile speculation, for we can live in faith. We know God and trust Him. That is enough!

6

Quiet Places in Heavy Traffic

Some people reject the Christian faith because they cannot harmonize its concept of a good God with the terrible conditions they see in the world. This was illustrated in an editorial I read years ago. The author, a leading socialist, said that the poverty and squalor of the slums and the constant threat of global war often made him weep. He said he wished that the good and omnipotent God described by the Christians really did exist. The writer declared that if he had the power the Bible ascribes to the Lord, he would quickly cure all crippling diseases, make right the injustices of society, and put an end to all human violence.

I imagine all of us at times have wished we had unlimited power. We feel helpless and frustrated in the presence of life's tragedies. We wish we could bring healing to all little children afflicted with terminal diseases, put a stop to crime, end all wars, and have everyone go to heaven without dying. At least, that is what we think we would do.

The harsh realities of life make it seem inconsistent to hold a starry-eyed concept of a loving heavenly Father who is also omnipotent. If God is truly loving and all-powerful, why doesn't He do something about all the suffering and evil around us? Unless we believe what the Bible says about sin entering the world, we have no way of harmonizing the idea of a good God with the conditions of society. The Scriptures provide us with a proper perspective, however, for they face life as it is, present a logical system of belief, and emphasize both God's holiness and His love.

When Solomon observed the terrible nature of injustice, the universality of death, and the predominance of unhappiness, he was deeply distressed. As he reflected upon these facts, a series of painful thoughts or goads came to his mind. In every case, however, the Lord revealed a nail of divine truth, which gave him peace of mind.

The Prevalence of Injustice

Conscientious, righteous men are perplexed by the fact that evil men often appear to be successful and happy while those who are honest and kind experience misfortune and misery. In fact, the Preacher was distressed that even the courts of the land, where justice should be done if in no other place, were being manipulated by heartless and unjust men. "And, moreover, I saw under the sun the place of justice, that wickedness was there; and the place of righteousness, that iniquity was there" (Ecc. 3:16).

In those days, as now, judges sometimes favored the rich. Lawyers would ardently defend a man and try to gain an acquittal even though they knew he was guilty. Verdicts of "innocent" were bought by bribery, and for a financial payoff witnesses would swear they saw something which never happened.

This deplorable situation, which has always existed in society, is an intellectual roadblock to faith for many people. It is difficult enough to harmonize belief in a good God with sin, suffering, and death; but it is even more perplexing when we see that everything is topsy-turvy—the wicked on top and the righteous on the bottom.

If only we could see every wrong quickly righted and every crime immediately and justly punished, we might conclude that the Lord has some beneficent purpose in mind. But all too often evil men are exalted and good people are despised. Dishonesty brings rewards, and integrity is penalized. No wonder many people are bewildered. *Where is this righteous God who is supposed to be ruling the universe?*

When an unsaved person begins to reflect upon these matters, his mind is sometimes goaded into a quest for truth. He wants to believe that it pays to be good. He would like to think that in the end righteousness will be vindicated and a new day of justice will dawn. But the hard, brutal facts of life oppose him. This causes him pain. It hurts when one is forced to conclude that life is cruel to the righteous and kind to the ruthless.

God Will Judge All

The nail of divine truth which solves these problems is now set forth: "I said in mine heart, God shall judge the righteous and the wicked; for there is a time there for every purpose and for every work" (Ecc. 3:17).

Solomon knew this by divine revelation, not

his own reasoning powers. Someone who dreams up his own religious system might decide that the Lord will deal righteously with everybody at a future time, but he cannot express this with confidence if he is honest in his observation of society. Only through the Scriptures can this be known with certainty.

The Hebrew people of that day did not possess the revealed truths about final judgment and eternity as clearly as they are set forth in the New Testament. But what they had was sufficient to give Solomon assurance regarding the future.

In the garden of Eden, God declared both His punishment for sin and His promise of redemption.

Though under the Law emphasis was upon earthly blessing or punishment, the idea of a future life is implicit throughout the Pentateuch. Enoch, who walked with God, was taken from earth without dying. The patriarchs were "gathered to their fathers" at death, and, as the eminent Hebrew scholar Delitzsch said, this was "a union of spirits, not of corpses."

The Psalms teach that God's righteousness will be manifested in a world beyond this one. In Psalm 17, for example, the inspired writer first expresses his dismay at the prosperity of the wicked, but then declares the temporal, short-lived nature of their success, saying they "have their portion in this life" (v. 14). He then makes the triumphant declaration, "As for me, I will behold Thy face in righteousness: I shall be satisfied, *when I awake, with Thy likeness*" (v. 15). He is speaking of awaking from the sleep of death at the time of resurrection. The believer will find satisfaction in the presence of God, but the wicked have no such prospect. Whatever happiness they find on this earth is all they will ever have.

Old Testament believers like Solomon, unaware of many details later made known by God, were assured that in the end the love and justice of the Lord would be manifested.

Today we live in the light of the full revelation of the New Testament, and therefore we have a far better concept of the final reckoning. Our Saviour declared that He will be the Judge in that ultimate decision. "For the Father judgeth no man, but hath committed all judgment unto the Son" (John 5:22).

The Apostle Paul taught that God "hath appointed a day, in which He will judge the world in righteousness by that Man [Christ] whom He hath ordained; concerning which He hath given assurance unto all men, in that He hath raised Him from the dead" (Acts 17:31). He also said that believers will stand at the "judgment seat of *Christ*" (2 Cor. 5:10).

The Apostle John portrayed the unsaved of all ages as they will appear before the *Son of God* at the great white throne (see Rev. 20:11-15). Thomas Carlyle, commenting on John's description of this final judgment, made the following statement: "What a magnificent conception is that of a last judgment! A righting of all the wrongs of the ages."

This is an awesome thought, and it gives great satisfaction to the sensitive person who loves God. The Lord Jesus will take every circumstance into account and judge accordingly. His just decisions will not be subject to appeal, for He is the Supreme Court of the universe. Every intelligent moral creature will someday bow to Jesus Christ, and in so doing will acknowledge His deity and absolute justice (see Phil. 2:9-11).

All Men Die Like Beasts

The Preacher was further goaded in his thinking by the observation that human beings and animals die alike, suffering similar death throes and leaving a repulsive corpse. "For that which befalleth the sons of men befalleth beasts. Even one thing befalleth them: as the one dieth, so dieth the other; yea, they have all one breath, so that a man hath no preeminence above a beast; for all is vanity. All go unto one place; all are of the dust, and all turn to dust again" (Ecc. 3:19-20).

These statements should not be taken as logical conclusions based upon Solomon's comments about the final judgment. Rather, they are observations made by the Preacher back when he was struggling in his own wisdom with the problems of existence. While going through this period of mental agony, he was troubled by the idea that maybe God lets men die in such a humiliating manner to teach us that we are nothing more than animals.

From a physical standpoint only, people and animals are similar in death. Both man and beast grow weaker, breathe with increasing difficulty, and finally expire. The corpse of a human being decomposes just as rapidly as that of any animal and is consumed by the same organisms.

It is indeed a humbling experience to see the dead body of a fellow human being before the mortician utilizes his skill upon it. A prominent minister said that he never felt more insignificant than the day he went into the morgue to identify the remains of a person he was told might be a member of his church. He said that if he had not been firmly convinced that man's uniqueness lies in the area of the spirit, he would have become morbid and terribly depressed.

It is painful for a person who does not know the Lord Jesus Christ to reflect deeply upon the subject of death. That is exactly why people do not even like to talk about it. So often a person may realize he is dying, but will not admit it to his loved ones. The family also knows, but carefully avoids all references to it. They discuss the weather, the scores of yesterday's ball games, and other trivia but steer the conversation away from the true situation. How tragic! Truly, thoughts about death and eternity sting like goads in the life of one who is not a Christian. They disturb and unsettle, and the tendency is to reject all such reflection.

Man's Spirit Lives On

Thinking about death is difficult for one who has no faith, but the believer can contemplate it without becoming distressed. He is convinced that although it may appear otherwise, man does not actually die like the animal. Solomon expressed this nail of truth when he said that the human spirit does not perish with the body. "Who knoweth the spirit of man that goeth upward, and the spirit of the beast that goeth downward to the earth?" (Ecc. 3:21)

Many present-day Bible students are influenced by liberal scholars who maintain that the idea of a life after death was unknown in Israel at the time Ecclesiastes was written, and therefore take this statement as an expression of uncertainty. They read this text, "Who knows *whether or not the spirit of man goes upward and the spirit of the beast goes downward at death?*" This makes the Preacher express doubt that there is any difference between the destinies of man and beast.

Many capable Hebrew scholars thoroughly disagree with this interpretation, however, and set forth excellent grammatical arguments for finding it unsatisfactory. Leupold, after a long and thorough discussion of the Hebrew text, suggests the following paraphrase: "There are not many who take to heart as they ought the fact that the spirit of man goeth upward, and that the spirit of the beast goeth downward to the earth" (*Exposition of Ecclesiastes,* cited earlier). This is really a declaration that few people grasp the truth that the destinies of a person and an animal are different. The Preacher's words, therefore, do not express uncertainty about life after death, but declare that most people lack understanding on this subject.

Consider again the words of Ecclesiastes 3:21, "Who knoweth the spirit of man that goeth upward, and the spirit of the beast that goeth downward to the earth." The animal's life goes "down," perishing with the body and no longer existing in any form. But the soul of a person goes "upward," suggesting that he goes on living. This is not to be taken as teaching that the soul of every human being goes to heaven at death, but that it does not go into the grave with the body. It continues to exist.

The Preacher expresses this truth more clearly in Ecclesiastes 12:7, where he says that at death the spirit returns to God who gave it, but the body returns to the dust. He is not discussing the matter of judgment and eternal destiny in either heaven or hell, just the fact that man's soul lives on after his body dies.

Although this nail of truth was comforting and brought a measure of hope to Old Testament believers, it did not contain the complete teaching of God on the subject of life after death. This is found in the New Testament. Today we have the advantage of possessing the record of our Lord's death, burial, resurrection, and ascension into heaven.

We are also blessed with further revelation regarding the state of the soul after death. Stephen, the first martyr of the church, was given a glimpse of heaven just before he died. Though condemned by an earthly court, he saw a vision of Jesus Christ standing before the Supreme Court of the universe as his Witness, Vindicator, and Advocate, ready to receive His faithful servant. No wonder this young deacon was able to pray for the forgiveness of his executioners and, while the stones were smashing into his body, could triumphantly shout, "Lord Jesus, receive my spirit" (Acts 7:59).

Death for the believer is victorious, for it is the time of going to be with Jesus. It may come quickly through an accident or a coronary attack, or more slowly by a long and painful disease, but in every case we can say with the Apostle Paul that to die is "to depart and to be with Christ, which is far better" (Phil. 1:23).

Live Joyously by Faith

Solomon now gives us a practical exhortation. He tells us that when we accept God's assurances by faith, we can live joyously and without worry. "Wherefore, I perceive that there is nothing better, than that a man should rejoice in his own works; for that is his portion. For who shall bring him to see what shall be after him?" (Ecc. 3:22).

When we do what is right, we feel good about life, ourselves, and God. We do not fret about injustices or brood about the unpleasant aspects of death. We do not have to "be anxious" about the future, and we can accept with thanks the good things God gives us. Our complete trust in Him lets us live serenely at all times.

The Preacher's expression "For who shall bring him to see what shall be after him?" is not a reference to eternity but to the future of life on this planet. Only God knows what lies ahead, so let us rely totally upon Him. This admonition is especially appropriate in our day, for people have never shown more anxious concern about the future than they do now. Millions are consulting astrologers and studying horoscopes. Thousands are avid readers of the works of self-appointed prophets and prophetesses. Among intellectuals a new science called "futurology" has attracted many prominent followers. Ecologists and conservationists scare us about the future. Men and women everywhere are afraid of what is going to happen.

But how wonderful to be a child of God! We need not fear the future! We know something about what will happen, for the Bible gives us a general outline of the course of events which will take place on earth when Christ returns.

What we don't know, we can leave with Him. The Scriptures declare that "the secret things belong unto the LORD" (Deut. 29:29), and that should be good enough for the Christian. We can therefore live our lives one day at a time, facing the perplexities as they come without plunging into despair.

The Unhappiness in Life
The third depressing enigma considered by Solomon is the fact that in a world with so much potential for enjoyment, so many people are desperately un-

happy. "So I returned, and considered all the oppressions that are done under the sun; and, behold, the tears of such as were oppressed, and they had no comforter; and on the side of their oppressors there was power, but they had no comforter! Wherefore, I praised the dead which are already dead more than the living which are yet alive. Yea, better is he than both they, which hath not yet been, who hath not seen the evil work that is done under the sun" (Ecc. 4:1-3).

The Preacher now is thinking of rich men who "wring perspiration and blood out of the poor" like squeezing water out of a sponge. In Solomon's day it was not uncommon for slaves to work from sunup to sundown every day of the week, to be beaten by cruel taskmasters, to be deprived of family life, and to receive only enough food to keep body and soul together. How unhappy the lot of these poor people! Even today we are disturbed when we think about the starvation, disease, and poverty the masses in many sections of the world must hopelessly endure because of the greed of those in power.

This observation hurts! It is a painful goad! The history of man is an inescapable record of the suffering of the poor while the wealthy sate themselves with every pleasure money can buy. No wonder so many agree with Solomon as he looked upon these terrible conditions from the vantage point of man "under the sun." It does often seem that people would be better off dead than alive. Yes, if one must spend his entire lifetime in wretchedness and poverty, it might be said that the Preacher was right. It would be good if such a person had never been born.

Dreadful unhappiness is not limited to the oppressed, however, for Solomon also sees it in the lives of many who achieve what the world terms "success." "Again, I considered all travail, and every right work, that for this a man is envied by his neighbor. This is also vanity and vexation of spirit" (Ecc. 4:4).

The meaning of this verse is expressed accurately in the New American Standard Bible: "And I have seen that every labor and every skill which is done is the result of rivalry between a man and his neighbor. This too is vanity and striving after wind."

A person who is continually trying to outdo his neighbor or fellowworker cannot be truly happy. All he is thinking about is making an impression on someone or outstripping his rival. Besides, the more he succeeds, the more certain it is that people will hate him. All too often temporal achievement brings increased animosity and envy rather than love and admiration. How empty a life of earthly success can be!

Solomon goes on to say that when a person reflects upon this truth, it is such a sharp goad that he may decide to "cop out" on life. "The fool foldeth his hands together, and eateth his own flesh" (Ecc. 4:5).

If you have nothing more than your own wisdom, maybe the best thing to do is to fold your hands and let yourself starve to death. Maybe this is a better pathway than to throw yourself into the corporate arena where successful men ruthlessly compete and the victors pay a dear price for every trophy they receive. In a highly competitive society, where pride and greed play such a large part, a person who attains success may have to both hate and be hated. What a miserable life if indeed it takes on such a character!

Quietness of Spirit Is Possible

The nail of revealed truth to answer the pain one feels when he reflects upon the unhappiness of mankind is the admonition that a quiet and restful spirit *can* be experienced through trust in God. "Better is an handful with quietness, than both the hands full with travail and vexation of spirit" (Ecc. 4:6).

Whether one lives under oppressive conditions or as a highly motivated top achiever, he can possess a spirit of quiet contentment. But this is possible only for the one who loves the Lord and trusts Him. How true the inspired words, "Better is little with the fear of the Lord, than great treasure and trouble therewith. Better is a dinner of herbs where love is, than a stalled ox and hatred therewith" (Prov. 15:16-17).

The exhortation to seek out the contentment which springs from a right relationship with God is repeated often in the Book of Ecclesiastes. It is indeed an important truth. When one is spiritually healthy, he can find satisfaction in life, for he can accept himself and his place in society. He is conscious that God has forgiven his sin, and that every aspect of life is ultimately under the Lord's control. By applying these principles to everyday conduct, believers can eliminate many of the tensions that cause ulcers and the anxieties which require the help of psychiatrists or psychologists.

Summary

Life is full of perplexing elements for which no one can find easy answers. It is hard to understand why unjust men often rise to places of prominence and influence. It sometimes looks as if the evolutionist may be right in saying that man and beast are basically the same, for physically they suffer and die alike. Then, too, the sum total of human unhappiness is staggering, for millions are oppressed and live in squalor, and the affluent are so often miserable because of the blighting effects of hatred and envy. All these facts of existence, when reflected upon, can be sharp goads that sting the mind.

But the nails of divine truth give assurance to the man who believes in the Lord. He knows that man and beast have different destinies. He is confident that God in the person of Christ will be the final Judge of every human being. He will ultimately make all things right. As the Christian prays for his fellowmen and demonstrates Christian love, he does so with the quiet confidence that God is on the throne of the universe, working out His purposes and moving history toward His predetermined goal. He gratefully accepts the blessings of life and finds enjoyment in them. He has learned the secret of true happiness!

7
Right Turns through Experience

Did you hear about the man who was hobbling around on crutches and explained that he had been kicked by his horse? He then added wryly, "That's the second time! The first time it was an accident. But when a man lets it happen twice, it's just plain stupidity." Yes, he should have learned from experience, but he was merely being human in his failure. Most of us can recall instances when we did something wrong, suffered the consequences, and then staged a repeat performance.

The fact remains, however, that experience is the best teacher. This is one way God instructs us about life. A child who breaks a toy and then cries about it learns he must be more careful with his possessions in the future.

Solomon came to the place in his life where he was willing to learn from experience. Though gifted with wisdom from God, he had foolishly sought satisfaction in the pleasures, accomplishments, and learning of men. But when he discovered their emptiness, he abandoned them and turned to God. He wondered why everybody did not learn from experience as he did, and in Ecclesiastes 4 he portrays two men who failed to benefit from the lessons of life.

Two Men Who Did Not Learn

The Preacher first introduces us to a wealthy miser who was lonely, dissatisfied, and unhappy. "Then I returned, and I saw vanity under the sun. There is one alone, and there is not a second; yea, he hath neither child nor brother; yet is there no end of all his labor, neither is his eye satisfied with riches, neither saith he, 'For whom do I labor, and bereave my soul of good?' This is also vanity, yea, it is heavy travail" (Ecc. 4:7-8).

This man apparently decided that he would make the acquisition of money the goal of his life. A person who becomes preoccupied with this monomania usually isolates himself from society. In our mind's eye, therefore, we see a lonely miser, working from morning till night day after day and hoarding his money. He is suspicious of everyone, for he has the idea that people are being friendly to him only to gain a share of his wealth. He becomes surly, withdrawn, and despondent.

Solomon declares that this pathetic recluse had no relative to whom he could leave his money—not even a brother or a sister. But he continued this wretched pattern of living, never stopping to ask why. The old miser refused to learn from his experience. It disturbed Solomon, as it does us, to think that a man could be so foolish. What a tragedy!

Solomon then describes a second man who did not learn from experience. This time it is a king. We do not know whether or not the Preacher had a specific historical incident in mind, but that really matters very little. "Better is a poor and a wise child than an old and foolish king, who will no longer be admonished. For out of prison he cometh to reign; whereas also he that is born in his kingdom becometh poor" (Ecc. 4:13-14).

What the inspired writer describes certainly has happened many times throughout history. A poverty-stricken young man, with a background of imprisonment and trouble seized the opportunity to become king of the land. His success was due in part to a willingness to listen to the people, to heed wise counsel, and to strive to please his fellowmen.

Such a rapid rise to power was an oft-repeated phenomenon in the Oriental world of that day. When the citizens of the land grew discontented with a king who no longer showed concern for them, they would depose him and turn to a younger man who vowed to be different. But soon after he became established on the throne, the promising young ruler would often fall into the same pattern as his predecessors and forget the people who put him in office. He did not learn the lessons experience should have taught him. Asserting his authority with a disdain for others and their counsel, he subsequently lost power, was reduced to poverty and forgotten.

The fourth chapter of Ecclesiastes concludes like so many others with the pessimistic refrain, "Surely this also is vanity and vexation of spirit." The Preacher was sad because he had discovered the truth of the dictum, "The only thing we learn from history is that we don't learn from history." This was a painful goad.

Don't Go It Alone

When Solomon saw the unwise actions of these two men, he was goaded to seek the Lord for "nails of truth." God delivered to his understanding two helpful principles as wise counsel. The first of these is the insight that it is far wiser to associate with fellow human beings than to try to make it alone, living a self-centered and solitary life.

The lonely miser did not learn the lesson God was trying to teach him through experience. The Preacher, however, clearly understood the truth the Lord was setting forth. A man who lives wholly for selfish interests will never find lasting happiness. True joy can come only to one who relates himself to others in friendship and love. Companionship is better than isolation, and joint labor produces greater returns than that done alone. "Two are better than one, because they have a good reward for their labor" (Ecc. 4:9).

Three Examples

The Preacher underscored the teaching that man should associate with his fellowmen by citing three common experiences. He notes first that when two people walk together and one falls, the other can help him to his feet. "For if they fall, the one will lift up his fellow. But woe to him that is alone when he falleth; for he hath not another to help him up" (Ecc. 4:10). People of that day often traveled on paths that were rocky and uneven, and wore long robes in which their feet became entangled when they fell. They often walked many miles in a day and became exceedingly weary. This was therefore an appropriate and significant example.

Solomon's second illustration also centers upon two travelers in the Middle East. "Again, if two lie together, then they have heat; but how can one be warm alone?" (Ecc. 4:11) In this desert land, days were hot, but the nights became cold. Public sleeping quarters were unheated, and the latticed windows allowed the cold air to come in. The beds were only mats on the floor, and no blankets were provided, so the only protection was the wayfarer's outer garment. The people would therefore huddle together to stay warm, and one who was alone would lie shivering.

The third example is probably a continuation of the second. Solomon says that a man who journeyed alone was far more likely to be robbed than one who had a companion. In fact, the Preacher implies that the larger the company, the greater the degree of safety, for he quotes this well-known proverb of his day: "A threefold cord is not quickly broken" (Ecc. 4:12). This is similar to our current saying, "In unity there **is** strength." Everyone is aware that three strands woven together are more than three times as strong as a single one. Similarly, human experience shows that a group of people working together are far more effective than the same number when each goes his separate way.

These simple illustrations from Solomon's day which show the advantage of associating with others are supported by the general teaching of the entire Bible. The Scriptures tell us that man's most significant relationships, besides that with God, are with the family, society, and the church. It would be well here to take a look at each of these.

The Family

The creation story provides the basis for the truth that a person living by himself is incomplete and unfulfilled. It portrays Adam naming the animals and observing that they had mates, and makes the significant comment, "But for Adam there was not found an help fit for him" (Gen. 2:20). The progenitor of the human race, though living in a beautiful garden where he could have daily fellowship with God and observe many animals, became conscious of a missing dimension in his own life

Man experiences the full development of his personality only when he shares love, trust, and devotion with someone else. God therefore inaugurated marriage. In this relationship two people can respond to one another with understanding and love, share life's responsibilities, and experience both physical and psychological fulfillment.

Marital oneness is further enhanced through the birth of children. In fact, the home where love reigns is more like Paradise than any other place in today's world. Both the Old and New Testaments place great emphasis upon love, faithfulness, and submission within the family structure. The man or woman who withdraws from parents and siblings, mate or children and seeks to live only for self cannot help but be lonely and unfulfilled. And the person who uses others for the gratification of his own sensual desires also transgresses the divine plan. The voice of experience tells mankind that love-filled homes are an essential element in a well-ordered society.

Society

Man is a social being, and God established government for the regulation of community life. The repeated declarations of the Bible indicate that we are to be honest, fair, and kind in our relationships with others.

The Lord commanded the Israelites to make provision for the poor by letting the corners of the field lie uncut, and by leaving gleanings in the vineyard. He forbade stealing, lying, or holding back a man's rightful wages. The Lord also gave laws for the protection of the deaf, the blind, and the poor, and told the people of Israel that each man was to love his neighbor as himself (see Lev. 19:9-18).

Jesus declared that the second table of the Ten Commandments can be summed up in the charge, "Thou shalt love thy neighbor as thyself" (Matt. 22:39). Because men and women have a low regard for government and refuse to accept their God-given responsibility for others, our world is filled with crime, starvation, and injustice.

The Church

Although the Gospel's demands are extremely personal, it is significant that the New Testament places much importance on the "fellowship of the saints." The word *koinonia*, used many times by the Apostle John, emphasizes the fact that believers in Christ are *partners* with one another, *sharers* of everything that comes to us through the Lord Jesus.

Paul makes numerous references to believers as members of the "body of Christ." He describes our interdependence by comparing us with the eyes, hands, feet, and other parts of the human body. Just as each is an essential part of the whole, and cannot get along without the others, so we must fulfill our roles within the Church (1 Cor. 12).

Peter spoke of Christians as "living stones" built into a spiritual house, thus emphasizing the truth that we do not stand alone, but unite with our fellow-believers in purpose and aim.

The biblical teaching about the family, the state, and the church confirms the voice of experience— no one should try to go it alone. A person is not complete in and of himself. God made us social beings who cannot find fulfillment without fellowship with Him and one another. The man who tries to live in solitude, making himself the center and circumference of all his desires, will never find joy, satisfaction, and true peace.

Proper Worship

Regular and sincere worship of the Lord is the best way the believer can keep his priorities properly aligned. Solomon teaches this when he declares that people who go to the Temple must be careful to offer prayers that truly come from their hearts, and to keep the vows they make. "Keep thy foot when thou goest to the house of God, and be more ready to hear, than to give the sacrifice of fools; for they consider not that they do evil" (Ecc. 5:1).

Think back to the gloomy picture of the lonely miser and the king who was deposed. Solomon had seen so many similar occurrences that it became depressing for him to think about it. The selfishness and pride of men led them into the same mistakes generation after generation. Why? Because they were sinners and slaves of their own passions, needing God's help.

The Preacher found by experience that life's depressing situations can be viewed from a new perspective when one engages in sincere worship. Life comes into proper focus, joy and optimism abound, and failure is avoided by regular communion with God.

In directing his reader's attention to the worship in the Temple, Solomon echoed the admonition in Psalm 73. Here Asaph first described his inner turmoil and bitterness as he thought about the prosperity of wicked men while he, an obedient and clean-living believer, was forced to endure severe affliction day after day. But he said that when he went to the Temple, he saw things differently. He could see that life was under the administration of God, and once again could view it from the standpoint of eternity. "When I thought to know this, it was too painful for me, until I went into the sanctuary of God; then understood I their end. Surely, Thou didst set them in slippery places; Thou castedst them down into destruction (Ps. 73:16-18).

Sincere worship delivered the psalmist from fretfulness, irritation, and peevishness. Through fellowship with God he was reminded that all his needs were supplied, and was confident that even death cannot break the love-forged link between his soul and the Almighty. "Whom have I in heaven but Thee? And there is none upon earth that I desire beside Thee. My flesh and my heart fail, but God is the strength of my heart, and my portion forever" (Ps. 73:25-26).

A proper view of self, God, and the world is restored when one comes to the house of the Lord for worship. This must be done in a correct spirit, and Solomon sets forth two essentials to insure success.

Be Sincere in Worship

His first directive is the admonition that offerings and prayers must be brought in sincerity. "Keep thy foot when thou goest to the house of God, and be more ready to hear, than to give the sacrifice of fools; for they consider not that they do evil. Be not rash with thy mouth, and let not thine heart be hasty to utter any thing before God; for God is in heaven, and thou upon earth; therefore let thy words be few. For a dream cometh through the multitude of business, and a fool's voice is known by multitude of words" (Ecc. 5:1-3).

Many of the men in Israel, preoccupied with their efforts to gain wealth, brought sacrifices only because they knew it was expected of them. They would offer prayers that were nothing more than a series of memorized formulas, repeating the same words again and again without giving any thought to what they were saying. The Preacher warned them to remember that they were addressing Almighty God, and instructed them to speak only that which came from the heart.

All of us are sometimes guilty of the same offense. We may attend a worship service, singing the hymns and joining in prayers, and yet have our thoughts far away, centered upon secular and earthly concerns. We casually place our money in the offering plate, forgetting that it ought to be presented with a thankful heart and with the earnest prayer that God will use it for His glory. Words without thought and offerings without gratitude! And that in the presence of the great Creator of the universe who gave His Son for our salvation!

Keep Your Vows

Solomon's second exhortation had to do with the making of vows. "When thou vowest a vow unto God, defer not to pay it; for He hath no pleasure in fools. Pay that which thou hast vowed. Better is it that thou shouldest not vow, than that thou shouldest vow and not pay. Suffer not thy mouth to cause thy flesh to sin; neither say thou before the angel, that it was an error. Why should God be angry at thy voice, and destroy the work of thine hands? For in the multitude of dreams and many words there are also many vanities; but fear thou God" (Ecc. 5:4-7).

Under the law, an Israelite was not obligated to make such vows to God. They were purely voluntary. But when men are in places of extreme difficulty, they are inclined to make rash promises to the Lord. Often the pledge is forgotten as soon as the crisis has passed.

Then, too, a person may say he will do something requiring great effort or sacrifice just to make a big impression upon those around him. Promises like this are seldom made good.

When people recklessly make vows and break them with equal abandon, they reveal an inadequate concept of God's holiness and majesty. The Preacher had discovered that God is to be feared, and said that it is better not to vow at all than to make pious promises and fail to keep them.

Solomon then warns the person who has made a hasty vow that if the priest reminds him of his neglect, he must not think that he can offer a little sacrifice and placate God. (Most commentators agree that the reference to the *angel* in verse 6 actually designates the priest who as God's messenger rebukes the Israelite for having broken his vow.) This attitude, which assumes that God can be easily appeased by empty ritualism is reprehensible in the Lord's sight. Any person who takes this position is sure to face God's judgments. The Lord is angry when people conceive of Him as a capricious deity who acts without principle or is pleased with meaningless ceremony.

Stop for a moment and take a look at your own life. Perhaps you have made a promise to God in a time of difficulty, and forgotten it now that the crisis is over. Maybe you have sung words of tremendous devotion to the Lord, telling Him that you will give Him your time, your service, your earthly goods, and even yourself. If you have not given serious thought to the words that flowed so glibly from your lips, heed the warning of Solomon. A song by Dick Anthony entitled "Will You Keep That Vow?" * beautifully expresses this admonition.

> Many years ago in a time of woe,
> To the Saviour a promise you gave;
> If He just would show you the way to go,
> You'd receive Him, your soul to save.
>
> In a time of pain when all hope seemed vain,
> You remember your promise to God;
> With your life sustained, and your health
>   regained,
> You would serve Him at home or abroad.
>
> Will you keep that vow to the Saviour now,
> The old promise that was broken somehow?
> So before Him bow and His will allow,
> Will you keep, will you keep that vow?

The Preacher then sums up his exhortations to worship sincerely. He says that when people talk freely about idle dreams as if they were messages from God, or pour forth a torrent of formal prayers which do not come from the heart, their devotion is empty of meaning in the Lord's sight. He calls upon men to fear God. They are to approach Him with such reverence and awe that they speak only that which they mean and promise only that which they intend to carry out.

In conclusion, the dead-end streets of failure and

---

disappointment can be avoided by the person who heeds the lessons of experience. The lonely miser did not learn the folly of his ways. Though wretched and alone, he persisted in his solitary and selfish manner of life until he died. The ambitious and capable young king likewise did not learn. At first he conducted himself wisely and listened to good advice, but after he was established in his position he became just like the king he deposed, and he too eventually lost his throne. Even kings do not benefit from others' mistakes. How sad that so many seem to copy these men! It hurts to see that few people ever really learn!

This goads our minds to seek further truth, and the Bible has supplied it in the "nails" of this chapter. Man was not created to live by himself. The Scriptures declare that he can find happiness, joy, and contentment only in a life of fellowship and love with others. He is to participate in his church, take an active role in society, and maintain a warm relationship with his family.

God alone can redeem men from the bondage of their willful ways. The believer should regularly go to the house of God to present his offerings, to pray, and to express his devotion to the Lord. But he must be sincere, for God is angry when people show a low regard for Him. Worship offered in reverence to the Lord, and with a deep consciousness of one's sinfulness and need, will keep man's view of God and himself in proper perspective, and help him to avoid the dead-end streets of those who fail to learn from experience.

8

Riches and
Other
Road Hazards

People tend to think "happiness is" being just a little
higher on the ladder of success than others. Our
natural human pride likes the idea of surprising
our friends by telling them about a promotion at
work, showing them our new automobile, or invit-
ing them to be our guest in the house we always
wanted but thought we could never afford. We
know many of the world's most famous and
wealthy people are unhappy, but somehow we
think it would be different with us. After all, we
are only asking for a little more prestige and money
than we now have!

According to Solomon the increase of power and
money in and of itself can never provide real happiness. He learned this through his own bitter experience. He was the richest king of his day, and
had become world-famous for his great intelligence
and worthy accomplishments.

In Chapter 5 he emphasizes the dangers of seeking happiness through the acquisition of money
and power. When people make wealth or power

the single pursuit of their lives they are in danger of destroying their character in the process. Even if they achieve these goals, they may find themselves enslaved by a way of life that does not satisfy them. Finally, they may suddenly lose their position and money through some misfortune, after which they are likely to go through the rest of their lives feeling bitter and resentful. This is worse, the Preacher says, than knowing only hard work and poverty from childhood to the grave.

Wealth Can Destroy Character

The first peril to the materialistic man is the loss of honesty and integrity. The government leaders of Solomon's day were typical examples of how this can happen, and he said no one should be surprised by the graft and injustice he sees among political leaders. He implies that dishonesty is a constant danger men face when serving in public office. "If thou seest the oppression of the poor, and violent perverting of justice and righteousness in a province, marvel not at the matter; for he that is higher than the highest regardeth; and there are higher than they" (Ecc. 5:8).

He describes how government officials on every level keep an eye on one another to make sure they get their cut. The ninth verse says that the "profit of the earth" (money gained by taxation) is shared by everyone, and even the king makes certain he gets his portion.

The political ills the Preacher portrays here accurately describe governmental conditions during many periods of history. People are proud and greedy by nature, and that is why they manifest a lust for power and wealth. When they gain positions of responsibility and are given further opportunities to "get ahead," the temptation to deceive and be dishonest is often too much for them. Many a man who started his career in politics with a sincere dedication to high principles has gradually compromised his integrity to gain desirable ends.

Senator Mark O. Hatfield, in a speech delivered at a Chicago prayer breakfast in May, 1973, declared that the more prestige and power a man gains, the harder it is for him to admit he is wrong. He also tends to lose an awareness of his culpability before God. The Oregon statesman said that whenever power becomes the aim of a man's life, he unconsciously places himself above the laws of God and his fellowmen. The senator urged Christians to be aware of these perils of leadership, and to intercede in prayer for all who carry great responsibility in business, economics, and government. He reiterated his conviction that every man who has a prominent position is under the continual temptation to use all means available, both lawful and unlawful, to maintain and augment his power and prestige. He is in a place of grave moral danger!

Wealth Can Enslave

Solomon observed that the man who pursues wealth and prestige as his goals in life may easily become a slave to this quest. "He that loveth silver shall not be satisfied with silver, nor he that loveth abundance, with increase; this is also vanity. When goods increase, they are increased who eat them; and what good is there to the owners thereof, saving the beholding of them with their eyes? The sleep of a laboring man is sweet, whether he eat little or much; but the abundance of the rich will not suffer him to sleep" (Ecc. 5:10-12).

The more a man has, the more he wants. When a person reaches the next rung on the ladder of success, he is likely to adopt a life-style which eats up his increased income. The $60 car payment on a Ford Galaxie becomes $120 a month on a new Mercury Marquis. Add the installments on a new color television, and the family provider is right back where he started. Once again he says, "I wish I could earn a little more money. It's just impossible to make ends meet." He is like the judge who resigned a $30,000-a-year position to go into private practice because he could not live on his income any longer.

The wife of a prominent surgeon is desperately unhappy, even though she lives in a luxurious home and has all the money she needs. Her husband has been caught up in a vicious cycle of making and spending money, just so he can keep the reputation of being the most successful man in his field. He is irritable at home, unhappy with life, and frustrated with himself. Yet he continues on. He is like a man driving down a street which he realizes will come to a dead end, but he does not know how or where to get off.

The enslaving power of the "love of money" is vividly described in Ecclesiastes 6. "If a man beget an hundred children, and live many years, so that the days of his years be many, and his soul be not filled with good, and also that he have no burial; I say, that an untimely birth is better than he. Yea, though he live a thousand years twice told, yet hath he seen no good. Do not all go to one place? All the labor of man is for his mouth, and yet the appetite is not filled" (Ecc. 6:3, 6-7).

In these verses the Preacher first pictures a man to whom God gives long life and many children, but who becomes so bound by insatiable greed for riches that he leads a miserable existence. He then says that even if this man were to reach the impossible age of "a thousand years twice told," he would be worse off than if he had never been born. His worries about money and his fear that his descendants might not give him a proper burial in the ancestral tomb make life so miserable that even the lot of a stillborn child would be better. One who has never existed has been spared the agony this rich man experienced through all his long years. He was so bound to his lust for wealth and power that his life became a monotonous tale of woe.

Wealth Can Be Lost

Solomon's third critique points out that at best riches are an insecure possession, and that they could easily be lost in a bad venture. When this happens, the man who loves money suffers crushing grief. "There is a great evil which I have seen under the sun, namely, riches kept for the owner's thereof to their hurt. But those riches perish by evil travail; and he begetteth a son, and there is nothing in his hand. As he came forth of his mother's womb, naked shall he return to go as he came, and shall take nothing of his labor, which he may carry away in his hand. And this also is a great evil, that in all points as he came, so shall he go. And what profit hath he that hath labored for the wind? All his days also he eateth in darkness, and he hath much sorrow and wrath with his sickness" (Ecc. 5:13-17).

In this vivid picture we see a man who obtains great wealth, loses it through bad investments, and is reduced to absolute poverty. He had hoped to leave a fortune to his son, but now the boy is left with no inheritance. What a terrible disappointment! All this hard work down the drain! Though he had slaved for money, and was rich for a little while, he will go to the grave as poor as when he came into the world. Everything he lived for is gone. No wonder the Preacher says this man will live out his days in mental and spiritual anguish, never free from resentment, vexation, and remorse.

"Rags to riches" is a beautiful success story, but its opposite is a tragedy of the greatest magnitude. A lifetime of povery is far better than being rich and then losing it all. Many men and women have committed suicide because they could not stand the thought of losing their wealth and popularity after having been on top.

A few poor investments and a person's money may be gone. A few tough breaks, and a high position may be lost. If one lives for wealth or power, then suddenly loses them, he has nothing to live for. Think of what such a person must endure! Every time he eats a meal, he remembers the lavish table he used to spread when he invited large numbers of people to be his guests. Every time he sees a picture of the magnificent home in which he used to live, or drives past the houses of his erstwhile friends, he is overwhelmed with feelings of envy, bitterness, and anger. If he had never had money in the first place, he would be far happier now. Yes, one of the grave perils of wealth and position is the bitter unhappiness that follows if they are lost.

Trust God and Be Content

Having shown that riches often are more of a curse than a blessing, Solomon now drives home the nail of divine truth: A person who places his trust in God can enjoy the ordinary things of life. He will always be grateful to the Lord, no matter how much or how little he has. "Behold that which I have seen; it is good and fitting for one to eat and to drink, and to enjoy the good of all his labor that he taketh under the sun all the days of his life, which God giveth him; for it is his portion. Every man also to whom God hath given riches and wealth, and hath given him power to eat thereof, and to take his portion, and to rejoice in his labor; this is the gift of God. For he shall not much remember the days of his life, because God answereth him in the joy of his heart" (Ecc. 5:18-20).

Again the Preacher asserts that a believer, whether he be rich or poor, can obtain pleasure in eating, drinking, and the regular blessings of life, because he knows they come from his heavenly Father.

God is not an austere Being who dislikes it when His children are happy. He does not gain pleasure from tantalizing us by offering something that appears attractive but is harmful and disappointing when we get it. He has placed us on a planet that offers abundance, and He wants us to enjoy it. The hermits and ascetics had the mistaken idea that God is pleased when His children choose a life of hunger, privation, and needless suffering. On the contrary, the Lord is delighted when He sees a happy family. He is pleased when people joyously partake of the good things of this world. It is not His fault that men are greedy for wealth and power. He is not to blame when cravings or lusts drive them to destroy their own characters and bring misery upon themselves and their fellows.

For the one who knows the Lord, life can be wonderful even in spite of unpleasantness. Recognizing the perils and pitfalls of a self-centered life, the Christian gratefully accepts the good things he receives from God and finds joy as he shares them with others. In fact, the one who possesses true faith will be so caught up in his life of gratitude and praise to God that he will not be disturbed by the swiftly passing years. "For he shall not much remember the days of his life, because God answereth him in the joy of his heart" (Ecc. 5:20).

The peace a believer experiences when he lives in fellowship with the Lord is rich and complete. This makes it easy to live one day at a time. Outward circumstances are not the determining factor in his estimate of happiness. His life is centered upon God and His will. He lives each day in humble dependence upon his heavenly Father and trusts Him for tomorrow. Yes, the years roll on, but each day brings him nearer to his home in heaven.

In conclusion, the desire for riches and prestige, and the methods often required to gain them, carry perils that must not be minimized. Many people demolish their integrity and self-esteem in the process of obtaining materialistic goals. True happiness is impossible when greed and ambition dominate. Then, too, the lust for wealth and power enmeshes men in a futile round of earning and spending, even though they are not finding the satisfaction they expected. Finally, the person who obtains these longed-for ambitions and then loses them is worse off than if he had never been born.

For the man who walks with God, however, happiness is a way of life. He accepts the good things with gratitude, enjoys them, and trusts the Lord for tomorrow. His inner peace and gladness are more precious than all the pleasures money can buy. Yes, misfortune may rob him of his earthly riches, tragedy may take away his family, and disease may deprive him of health, but he will still be joyful.

The Preacher's contrast between the grief of the materialist who lost his wealth and the joy of the man who walks with God reminds us of Job. This patriarch lost his money and all his children in two rapid strokes, but was able to say, "Naked came I out of my mother's womb, and naked shall I return there. The Lord gave, and the Lord hath taken away; blessed be the name of the Lord" (Job 1: 21). Later, when boils broke out all over his body and his wife told him to curse God, and die, his faith stood strong, and he said, "Thou speakest as one of the foolish women speaketh. What? Shall we receive good at the hand of God, and shall we not receive evil?" (Job 2:9-10).

Yes, the person who walks in fellowship with God may be penniless, alone in the world, and in poor health, but his joy gives him more true riches and genuine power than the most wealthy and influential monarch in the world.

9

As You Travel, Ask God

The seventh chapter of Ecclesiastes has often been misinterpreted, especially by scholars who question the inspiration of the Scriptures. Let me cite two examples.

First, they take the Preacher's statements about being "not righteous overmuch" and "not wicked overmuch" as recommending a lukewarm devotion to God—the very thing Jesus so strongly condemned in Revelation 3:15-16.

Second, they interpret Solomon's comment that he could not find one good woman in a thousand as expressing the worst kind of male chauvinism. We may chuckle at such a remark, especially when we consider that Solomon had a thousand wives and concubines. We may even laugh to ourselves as we picture the reaction of a "women's libber" who reads what he said. But since we believe that Ecclesiastes belongs in the canon of Scripture, we must look upon these words as a serious discussion of basic spiritual issues.

Ecclesiastes 7 contains one predominating goad:

the pain, sorrow, and perplexity of existence cannot
be escaped. Though we possess a sense of the eternal, we are dying men and women in a world of
change and decay. This depressing fact is coun-
tered by a spike of divine truth: if we choose the
path of wisdom that comes from God rather than
the dead-end streets of human design, we will find
joy and meaning in life. Solomon lists specifically
nine preferred choices—*road signs to a happier and
more successful life.*

1. Choose Sobriety; Reject Frivolity

The Preacher begins by urging us to be serious,
not trifling, in our approach to life. His first statement appears extreme upon cursory examination,
but he goes on to explain exactly what he means.
"A good name is better than precious ointment; and
the day of death, than the day of one's birth. It is
better to go to the house of mourning, than to go to
the house of feasting; for that is the end of all men,
and the living will lay it to his heart" (Ecc. 7:1-2).

Solomon is not so sour on life that he considers
the birth of a baby to be a tragedy and a funeral
to be good fortune. Rather, the day of death is better than the day of birth *because of the lessons it
teaches.*

When a loved one dies, we are more inclined to
think of spiritual realities than when something
pleasant takes place. The atmosphere of a funeral
home affords many opportunities for spiritual reflection. When we stand alongside a casket, either
as a mourner or as a friend who comes to express
his condolences, we are reminded of the transitory
nature of earthly life.

At such times we feel keenly the supernatural
comfort and strength that comes from God, or we
sense the grief and despair that naturally arise

within the heart. Then again, we may observe God's grace in others, or see how inadequate man is to cope with the ultimate issues of life. Yes, at a funeral home, which Solomon calls the "house of mourning," we are taught many valuable lessons from the Lord which cannot be learned in any other way.

At a banquet or dinner party, by contrast, our attention is focused upon the pleasures and delights of this world. The atmosphere is light and gay, and serious topics are deliberately avoided. As noted previously, however, the Christian is not afraid to face life as it is. Solomon emphasizes that the believer can openly confront its grim realities and find great joy in everyday living as he gratefully accepts what comes from the Lord. But he must always see things from the proper perspective, and this can be obtained far more readily in a funeral home than at a dinner party.

The person who goes to the "house of mourning" will profit spiritually. "Sorrow is better than laughter; for by the sadness of the countenance the heart is made better" (v. 3). The unhappy faces and tear-filled eyes of the bereaved may be the means of producing deep inner joy, for the feelings that occur at the side of a casket can lead a person to accept God's salvation.

The character of the wise man is indicated by the statement of verse 4 that he is "in the house of mourning." This means that he has accepted the inevitability of death and is spiritually prepared to meet it. The fool, on the other hand, is shallow and irresponsible in his outlook, and spends his days "in the house of feasting" to escape the serious realities of existence (see Ecc. 7:4).

Some people will do anything to avoid going to

a funeral home. They express their condolences by mail or on the telephone. Although they excuse themselves by saying they can not stand the morbid atmosphere, in reality they are unwilling to look death squarely in the eye. If a loved one dies, they dull their senses with alcohol or tranquilizers before they dare view the body or greet the friends who come to express sympathy. They do not want to talk about anything really significant, but spend their time watching television, reading light novels, or just having fun. In this manner they sidestep situations calling for spiritual decisions.

The man who knows God, on the other hand, is willing to confront the solemn aspects of human experience. When he hears that a friend or relative is ill, he pays a call and discusses the serious aspects of life. When death invades the home of someone he knows, he is quick to minister to the sorrowing. When bereavement comes into his own family, he possesses an inner stability and peace which shows that he has learned well the lessons God teaches in "the house of mourning."

The choice is ours. We can either walk the dead-end streets of the frivolous, bound by fear of death and its consequences, or follow the thoroughfare of the sober-minded, confident man of faith

2. Prize a Rebuke; Scorn the Song of Fools

A second option is placed before us. We are far better off to accept a valid word of criticism than to be mesmerized by the mindless songs of the world. "It is better to hear the rebuke of the wise, than for a man to hear the song of fools" (Ecc. 7:5).

Nobody likes a reprimand, though we may react in various ways when one comes. We may be deeply hurt, or we may become angry. To join a jolly crowd where no one reminds us of our sins is a natural tendency. Yet a word of reproof can be of inestimable value.

I remember a minister saying that he would never forget a rebuke he received as a boy. While working in a store, he was given some obscene cartoons. When a Christian businessman entered, he showed the page to him, thinking he would share his amusement. But when the mature believer saw what it was, he threw it on the floor and said, "I'm disappointed that you, a young man who has professed faith in Christ, can think these pictures are funny. Looking at them can only harm you. Get rid of them, and tell the Lord you're sorry!"

Thinking back, the pastor could still vividly remember the mixed feelings of embarrassment, shame, and resentment that welled up within him. He was tempted to make a heated reply, but he knew the man was right. He admitted it, confessed his sin to the Lord, and never forgot the lesson he learned that day. An admonition of this kind may be difficult to accept, but it can be tremendously valuable.

How do you respond when you are given a rebuke? Perhaps you can accept it quite graciously when it comes from your pastor as he preaches God's Word in sincerity, but how about when someone tells you face-to-face that you are wrong? With some people, that is like lighting the fuse on a stick of dynamite, especially when they have no intention of changing.

In warning us against choosing the "song of fools" instead of a wise rebuke, Solomon goes on to make a striking comparison. He says "the laughter of the fool" is like the crackling of thorns in a fire. People in Palestine burned dried thorn bushes when they wanted a small amount of quick heat, but they knew they could not use such fuel to cook everything that required a high temperature over a sustained period of time.

Similarly, the merriment of the worldly crowd gives only temporary relief. It does not solve any problems or bring about a change for the better in a person's life-style. The rebuke of a godly man or woman is far more valuable. Again, the choice is ours: to learn from criticism or follow the tantalizing song of the Pied Piper down the dead-end street of empty gaiety.

3. *Be Patient; Don't Be Angry*

The third street sign posted by the Preacher warns people to choose patience in difficult situations rather than to become ill-tempered and snarlish. "Better is the end of a thing than the beginning thereof, and the patient in spirit is better than the proud in spirit. Be not hasty in thy spirit to be angry; for anger resteth in the bosom of fools" (Ecc. 7:8-9).

Under the pressure of a moment we often lose track of our long-range objectives. Our determination to be loving and patient disappears the first time some little thing goes wrong. Later, after we calm down from an angry blowup, we are sorry.

A father told his family for two months that they were going to have a happy and fun-filled vacation. But when they had to backtrack a few miles to pick up a suitcase one of the children had forgotten, he became infuriated and cursed the child. His frustration caused him to lose perspective, and he nearly ruined the holiday for everyone. If he had been patient, he would not have had to apologize later.

It is foolish to become angry every time things go wrong. You only harm yourself, and you certainly do not change or improve the situation. In addition, smoldering resentment and pent-up irritation are harmful to the body and rob you of the faculty of clear thought.

4. Accept God's Way—Don't Complain

Some Christians are bright and happy as long as things are going well, but complain bitterly when circumstances turn against them. In their unhappiness they think back to the favorable times, and can find nothing in the present worth smiling about. The Preacher says to them, "Say not thou, 'What is the cause that the former days were better than these?' For thou dost not inquire wisely concerning this" (Ecc. 7:10).

Yearning for the "good old days" is not realistic. God has not changed, and life is very little different now than it was then. Grumblers may have become far less tolerant over the years, or conveniently forgotten how they grumbled in days gone by. Rather than cheerfully accepting their current situation as part of God's good plan, they prefer to gripe and complain.

Solomon urges these people to put their trust in the wisdom of God, for He oversees all and has a good plan for His own. In this the believer will find a wellspring of patience and submission, and be happy in spite of what happens (see Ecc. 7:11-14).

The belief that God is working out His eternal purposes is a spiritual possession of far greater value than all the money in the world. The man of God sees both good times and bad as permitted by the heavenly Father for the eternal welfare of His children. True, he does not know exactly what will happen in the immediate future, but he is certain that God will triumph in the end. This assurance enables him to be joyful in the face of every difficulty. He can live day-by-day with a peace in his heart that the world cannot give.

5. *Choose Godliness; Avoid Self-righteousness and Sensualism*

Many people overreact when made aware of the injustices of life. The Preacher now recommends the right way to respond and warns against two wrong roads often taken when people observe events in the lives of others, both good and evil. "All things have I seen in the day of my vanity: there is a just man that perisheth in his righteousness, and there is a wicked man that prolongeth his life in his wickedness. *Be not righteous overmuch,* neither make thyself overwise. Why shouldest thou destroy thyself? *Be not wicked overmuch,* neither be thou foolish. Why shouldest thou die before thy time?" (Ecc. 7:15-17).

When people see godly men die young and the wicked live in comfort to a ripe old age, they tend to fall into one of two errors—self-righteousness or sensualism.

First, some conclude that everyone who goes to an early grave somehow must have fallen short of doing what pleases the Lord. Therefore they set about to make up this lack in their own lives by extreme legalism, ascetic practices, or some other form of works-righteousness.

This way of thinking was typified by the Pharisees, who imposed literally thousands of picayunish laws upon the people. Yet their lives were marked by a sickening artificiality, and their theology was all wrong because they taught salvation by works. That was why Jesus referred to them ironically as the "ninety and nine righteous persons, who need no repentance" (Luke 15:7).

I like the comment of A. R. Fausset, "There cannot be *overmuch* of the righteousness that is by faith. But there is overmuch of the righteousness that consists in punctiliousness as to external ordinances, when these are substituted for 'the weightier matters of the law: judgment, mercy, faith, and love of God' (Matt. 23:23; Luke 11:42); and when they blind a man to his utter guiltiness" (Fausset, *Critical, Experimental, and Practical Commentary,* Eerdmans Publishing Co., Grand Rapids, Mich.).

The second wrong reaction is that of going down the road of lustful living, giving oneself over to unbridled sensuality. When Solomon says "Be not wicked overmuch," he is not implying that we may be a little bit wicked. No, indeed! He is merely setting up the antithesis to the other peril of self-righteousness. Many who see apparently good people suffer adversity or die young go down the pathway of a false and artificial works-religion while others go down the road of unrestrained wickedness. Both courses will lead to disaster.

6. *Exercise Self-restraint; Reject the Natural Impulse*

The sixth wise choice recommended by Solomon involves adopting the right attitude toward public opinion. It is natural to want to know what people are saying about us, and to be upset when the remarks are negative. But we are warned, "Take no heed unto all words that are spoken, lest thou hear thy servant curse thee" (Ecc. 7:21). Should a master eavesdrop on the conversation of his servants, he might hear them say things which will either crush his ego or lead him to react rashly.

God is honored when we always take as the overriding consideration, "What is right?" rather than "What will people say?" Then, too, if we do find out that people are slandering us, we must restrain the impulse to defend ourselves or to retaliate. We are to remember that we ourselves have been guilty of doing to others what they do to us. That is why Solomon adds, "For oftentimes also thine own heart knoweth that thou thyself likewise hast cursed others" (Ecc. 7:22). Therefore, turn to God in prayer, confess your own weaknesses and sins, and ask Him for grace to live above the natural inclinations.

7. *Follow God's Truth; Renounce Faith in Human Wisdom*

When standing at the crossroads, take the route marked out by God's revelation. Stay off the crowded road of human wisdom that leads nowhere! The inspired writer undoubtedly remembered the days when he tried to solve life's problems through secular wisdom, and now he contrasts the truth that comes from God with the speculations that originate in the minds of men.

He portrays human philosophy as a lewd, seductive woman who repeatedly entices men to follow her, then leads them to shame and despair. "All this have I proved by wisdom; I said, 'I will be wise,' but it was far from me. That which is far off, and exceedingly deep, who can find it out? I applied mine heart to know, and to search, and to seek out wisdom, and the reason of things, and to know the wickedness of folly, even of foolishness and madness; and I find more bitter than death the woman whose heart is snares and nets, and her hands as bands; whoso pleaseth God shall escape from her, but the sinner shall be taken by her" (Ecc. 7:23-26).

A careful reading of verses 23-25 establishes the

fact that Solomon is discussing the quest for human wisdom, not the dangers of fast women. He says that when he thought he could gain an understanding of life through study, he found the solution to be "far from me" and "exceedingly deep." Following the pattern established in Proverbs, he speaks of the woman "whose heart is snares and nets." To view these verses as only a warning against harlots is to do an injustice to the context.

Solomon is presenting us with a comparison. Even as a man who has been beguiled by an evil woman may afterward say that the consequences are worse than death, so the person who succumbs to the allurements of man's wisdom may suffer the same bitter pangs of remorse.

The terms *snares and nets* and *bands* used to describe the woman suggest the fact that human wisdom binds a person to a thought system that leads to hell. This warning applies to our day more than ever before. Existentialism, the prevailing philosophy of contemporary man, has plunged many people over the brink of despair. One who has been trapped into this way of thinking must seek deliverance by calling upon the Lord, for he can never break free through his own strength or intelligence.

The Preacher rounds off his discussion of the superiority of the wisdom that comes from God by saying, "Lo, this only have I found, that God hath made man upright; but they have sought out many devices" (Ecc. 7:29). According to the first three chapters of Genesis, God made man in His own image. Colossians 3:10 and Ephesians 4:24 tell us that man originally possessed true knowledge, righteousness, and holiness, but through sin he lost these qualities. Now the entire human race has gone astray, resorting to a variety of "devices" in a vain attempt to find satisfaction. But every philosophical system man devises becomes a dead-end street. The only way he can enter the pathway that leads to heaven is by acknowledging the failure of his own wisdom and accepting the Gospel of Jesus Christ.*

8. *Be Submissive; Don't Be Rebellious*

The Preacher's next word of instruction is a call for a submissive spirit instead of rebellion. He seems to be speaking about our responsibility toward an earthly ruler, though many commentators give excellent grammatical and linguistic reasons for seeing his language as metaphorical, and as referring to God, the ultimate King of the earth.

"Who is as the wise man? And who knoweth the interpretation of a thing? A man's wisdom maketh his face to shine, and the boldness of his face shall be changed. I counsel thee to keep the king's commandment, and that in regard of the oath of God. Be not hasty to go out of his sight. Stand not in an evil thing; for he doeth whatsoever pleaseth him. Where the word of a king is, there is power; and who may say unto him, 'What doest thou?' Whoso keepeth the commandment shall feel no evil thing; and a wise man's heart discerneth both time and judgment" (Ecc. 8:1-5).

Whether we take these words as referring to our obligation to earthly rulers or to the Lord, the

* The words to which we alluded in the introduction of this chapter, "One man among a thousand have I found," may relate to Solomon's experience while he was searching for a satisfactory philosophy of life through his own wisdom. He may be saying that he is the one man in a thousand who finally came to the truth, but that not one woman of all his worldly-wise associates ever found peace. It is certainly not an assertion that women are inherently more evil than men or that none of them is capable of salvation.

point is the same. Believers are to be characterized by a respectful and obedient attitude toward all who have authority. God has established echelons of command in the home, the church, society, and government, and the Christian must submit to all rightful authority as *unto the Lord.*

Sometimes we may be treated unfairly, but even then compliance is the response that is "acceptable with God." Listen to Peter's admonition written by the inspiration of the Holy Spirit. "Submit yourselves to every ordinance of man for the Lord's sake, whether it be to the king, as supreme, or unto governors, as unto them that are sent by him for the punishment of evildoers, and for the praise of them that do well. . . . Servants, be subject to your masters with all fear; not only to the good and gentle but also to the perverse. For this is thankworthy, if a man *for conscience toward God* endure grief, suffering wrongfully. For what glory is it if, when ye are buffeted for your faults, ye shall take it patiently? But if, when ye do well and suffer for it, ye take it patiently, *this is acceptable with God*" (1 Peter 2:13-14, 18-20).

9. *Prepare for Death; Don't Ignore It*

Many live as if they will be here on earth forever. Even people in their 70s and 80s will refuse to discuss spiritual realities, centering all their interest upon material possessions and secular pleasures. They boast about their accomplishments and continue to plan for this life, all the while ignoring their total helplessness in the face of death.

Such people would do well to heed this solemn warning: "For he knoweth not that which shall be; for who can tell him when it shall be? There is no man that hath power over the spirit to retain the spirit; neither hath he power in the day of death.

And there is no discharge in that war, neither shall wickedness deliver those that are given to it" (Ecc. 8:7-8).

No one has control over his spirit. When it comes his time to die, die he must. For all his arrogance, man still falls before the steady onslaughts of the grim reaper. The inevitability of death is emphasized by the use of a metaphor. The sinner is portrayed as a soldier in an army surrounded by the enemy and facing certain death. Even so is man. Though he plunges himself into a wicked life in an effort to avoid thinking about reality, this will not ultimately help him. Death must come, and he should prepare for it now.

The most important issue you will ever face is that of your own personal preparation for the life beyond. God has revealed in the Bible how to get ready for eternity. He has sent His Son, the Lord Jesus Christ, to make redemption possible. His sinless life, His crucifixion on Calvary's cross, and His resurrection from the grave were accomplished *for you.* Your faith in Christ will bring to you forgiveness of sins and the surety of eternal life. How foolish to ignore God's salvation! "For God so loved the world, that He gave IIis only begotten Son, that whosoever believeth in Him should not perish, but have everlasting life" (John 3:16).

The person who has placed his trust in Christ knows that death's power is broken, and is certain that he is on the road to heaven. What a glorious way to live!

A believer, however, is still confronted with the responsibility to make the better choices day by day. A successful and joy-filled life is conditioned upon continual fellowship with God and obedience to His Word. That is why Solomon has given us the nine specific directives discussed in this chapter to guide us. We must choose to be serious-minded and helpful to others rather than frivolous and shallow. We are wise to heed the word of deserved rebuke and not to evade reality through the giddy entertainment of the world. We must be patient as we trust God's wisdom and love, and not give in to anger. We are to walk the path of true godliness, and not become involved in acts of self-righteousness or fleshly indulgence. We must exercise self-restraint as we think of what people might be saying about us. We must be marked by a spirit of humble submission as we walk in obedience to the Lord.

Your happiness and peace of heart depend upon the choices you make. Let me urge you to choose the way of God. When you accept Christ as your Saviour, you are on the path that gives you a joyful life here on earth and leads to heaven. Then, as you make daily decisions in accordance with the principles of God's Word, you will avoid the dead-end streets of the man of the world, and will experience the delights of the walk of faith.

10

In the Dark, Follow the Son

"If I couldn't look at my present circumstances from the perspective of faith, I would be in favor of euthanasia. I would wish that my husband and I could be put to sleep immediately. But I'm thankful that I know God is going to take care of us, and I'm not really unhappy." These words came from the lips of an articulate 80-year-old Christian woman.

Her pastor could readily understand why she said these things. Her health was rapidly failing. Her husband, who had physical problems requiring care she no longer had strength to give, was senile and difficult to manage. She knew a nursing home would be best for both of them, but he would interpret such a suggestion as an indication that she did not love him anymore.

What a difficult situation! Yet this aged saint could smile, for she viewed life from the pinnacle of her solid belief in God's goodness!

The Christian can transcend the tangled, confusing maze of life's complex demands, and see clearly from the vantage point of faith. As a traveler going through the humid lowlands is encouraged by the sight of his summer home nestled in the mountain just ahead, so the believer can envision the eternal goal toward which the Lord is leading him. This gives meaning to his present confidence for the future.

Solomon stressed the value of faith's perspective in Ecclesiastes 8:9 through 9:18. Though man is repeatedly frustrated by the goads of his own proscribed vision, he can find the way by consulting the road map of God's revelation.

The First Goad: Crime Seems to Pay

In this section the Preacher raises an age-old problem. It looks as if the person who is dishonest gets farther than the one who maintains high standards. "All this have I seen, and applied my heart unto every work that is done under the sun; there is a time wherein one man ruleth over another to his own hurt. And so I saw the wicked buried, who had come and gone from the place of the holy, and they were forgotten in the city where they had so done; this is also vanity. Because sentence against an evil work is not executed speedily, therefore the heart of the sons of men is fully set in them to do evil" (Ecc. 8:9-11).

Solomon sees one man oppressing or taking advantage of another; yet this wicked man mingles with honorable people as if he were one of them. After a lifetime of worldly success, he dies, is buried, and people forget how cruel and evil he has been. The fact that he seems to have gotten away with his sin encourages others to be bold to do evil. Yes, all too often it looks as if it does not pay to be decent.

The First Nail: Appearances Can Be Deceiving
The Preacher counters this mistaken idea by a simple and straightforward affirmation of his faith in God. "Though a sinner do evil an hundred times, and his day be prolonged, yet surely I know it shall be well with them who fear God, who fear before Him; but it shall not be well with the wicked, neither shall he prolong his days, which are as a shadow, because he feareth not before God" (Ecc. 8:12-13).

A man may go on his sinful ways for many years, but the man of faith is not overwhelmed or dismayed by appearances. He knows the wicked will surely be punished and the righteous vindicated. Deep in his heart he is assured of the truth expressed in this poem by Stopford A. Brooke:

Three men went out one summer night,
No care had they or aim,
And dined and drank.
"Ere we go home
We'll have," they said, "a game."
Three girls began that summer night
A life of endless shame,
And went through drink, disease, and death
As swift as racing flame.
Lawless and homeless, foul, they died;
Rich, loved, and praised, the men:
But when they all shall meet with God,
And justice speaks—what then?
(from A. H. Strong's *Systematic Theology*)

The Apostle Paul emphasizes God's dealing with evil men in Romans. He writes: "But after thy hardness and impenitent heart treasurest up unto thyself wrath against the day of wrath and revelation of the righteous judgment of God, who will render to every man according to his deeds" (Rom. 2:5-6).

The Second Goad: Enjoy Life While You Can

Once again the Preacher drops down to the level of human reasoning concerning the perplexities of life. He expresses a philosophy common to many: eat, drink, and be merry, for tomorrow you die. "Then I commended mirth, because a man hath no better thing under the sun, than to eat, and to drink, and to be merry; for that shall abide with him of his labor the days of his life, which God giveth him under the sun" (Ecc. 8:15).

This conclusion is drawn from the reasoning expressed in verse 14, "There is a vanity which is done upon the earth, that there are just men, unto whom it happeneth according to the work of the wicked; again, there are wicked men, to whom it happeneth according to the work of the righteous; I said that this also is vanity."

Everyone who has presented the Gospel often on a personal level to the unsaved has encountered some who have said, "I see so little evidence of God's goodness and righteousness in the world that I'm not going to take a chance on giving up earth's pleasures and becoming a Christian. I'm going to enjoy the life I have now, because as far as I know it's the only one I'll ever have." They live by the maxim, "You only go around once, so grab all the gusto you can get."

The Second Nail: Acknowledge Your Finiteness

When you talk with a person who expresses this philosophy of life, a good way to respond is to begin by acknowledging that you do not know all the answers, but that you still trust God. We have all observed happenings for which we could find no logical explanation or justification. Sometimes it is best to admit that we do not know everything.

Here is what Solomon said in response to the "eat, drink, and be merry" attitude. "When I applied mine heart to know wisdom, and to see the business that is done upon the earth (for also there is that neither day nor night seeth sleep with his eyes), then I beheld all the work of God, that a man cannot find out the work that is done under the sun, because, though a man labor to seek it out, yet he shall not find it; yea, further, though a wise man think to know it, yet shall he not be able to find it" (Ecc. 8:16-17).

When you tell someone you do not understand all of God's ways, you are not weakening your Christian testimony. Every scientist makes the same admission regarding his area of study. Oppenheimer said that as we face the ocean of knowledge to be gained, what we understand now is but a cupful by comparison.

Scientific research and endeavor have become exceedingly specialized. A university student seeking his doctorate in chemistry said recently that when he came upon a problem he could not solve, he consulted four professors before he found one who was knowledgeable in that particular aspect of the subject. Every scholar who is honest will frankly admit that there is much he does not comprehend. Why can't we as Christians make the same admission?

The believer lives in peace, even with the awareness of his limitations, because he leaves matters in the hands of God. He is assured that the Almighty has a good plan which is consistent with His perfect wisdom, holiness, and love. How true the words of Paul, "Oh, the depth of the riches both of the wisdom and knowledge of God! How unsearchable are His judgments, and His ways past finding out!" (Rom. 11:33)

The person who views all of life from the vantage point of faith can say a hearty amen to this inspired exclamation. His faith in God makes it unnecessary for him to know all the answers. He trusts God. That is enough!

The Third Goad: Good and Bad Are Treated Alike

The Preacher, once again speaking from man's perspective only, points out that life does not favor good people over those who are evil. It uses everybody just about the same way: the righteous and the wicked, the religious and the ungodly, the man who tries to be truthful and the one who is unscrupulous. Then, in the end, all die alike. But it is better to be alive than dead, for at least the living can still have hope. To the man who ignores God's revelation, to be dead is to be gone and forgotten. In fact, Solomon says this situation gave rise to the proverb, "a living dog is better than a dead lion." This is the same as saying that one might better be a despised person and alive than be highly respected and dead (see Ecc. 9:1-6).

We must remember that the Preacher is expressing the viewpoint of one who believes in some kind of God but does not possess the truth as revealed in the Bible. He may acknowledge that an intelligent and powerful Being exists, but he does not see any evidence that moral conduct or religious devotion make any difference. To this deity, love and holiness have no meaning.

Omar Khayyam set forth such a belief when he spoke of a heartless, inexorable Fate which "dooms to slow decay or sudden death and to eternal oblivion all that is great, good, and beautiful in this world." In his dismal view we are:

But helpless pieces of a game he plays
Upon this checkerboard of nights and days;
Hither and thither moves, and checks, and slays,
And one by one back in the closet lays.

These pessimistic and gloomy words accurately represent the view of many non-Christians about life. They are goaded by the thought that if there is a God, He does not seem to care whether people live an upright life or not. Moral standards apparently mean nothing to Him, for good and bad get the same treatment. And finally, all must die and be lost in oblivion.

The Third Nail: Rejoice in God's Approval
The man of the world is lonely, wandering in the maze of life's perplexities, but the child of God can "live rejoicing every day." He knows he is the object of the Lord's loving attention and approval. "Go thy way, eat thy bread with joy, and drink thy wine with a merry heart; for God now accepteth thy works. Let thy garments be always white, and let thy head lack no ointment. Live joyfully with the wife whom thou lovest all the days of the life of thy vanity, which he hath given thee under the sun, all the days of thy vanity; for that is thy portion in this life, and in thy labor which thou takest under the sun" (Ecc. 9:7-9).

The Preacher again calls upon God's children to enjoy His good gifts and leave the worry to Him, but he adds a new perspective when he says, "God now accepteth thy works" (Ecc. 9:7). These words do not apply to just anybody. They can be said only of a person who is walking in obedience to the Lord.

God does *not* sanction the activities of a rebellious sinner. As the Preacher said in chapter 8, "It shall *not* be well with the wicked." The Old Testament saint, on the other hand, looking forward with the eye of faith to the coming Messiah, could be enthusiastic about life and give himself fully to the task of the day. He could live in confidence, for he knew his path was approved by the Lord.

The tenth verse reads, "Whatsoever thy hand findest to do, do it with thy might; for there is no work, nor device, nor knowledge, nor wisdom in Sheol, whither thou goest." This should not be construed as teaching nonexistence after death. The Preacher is simply affirming that as soon as we die, our opportunity for earthly service is ended. The labor we perform in this world and the intelligence we apply to the problems we confront will have no place in the afterlife. We must, therefore, view our time in this sin-cursed world as the opportunity to offer unique service to God even though we know heaven will be far better.

When we labor for Him, "redeeming the time," our brief sojourn here takes on great glory and significance. The Saviour expressed this thought beautifully when He said, "I must work the works of Him who sent me, while it is day; the night cometh, when no man can work" (John 9:4).

A minister had the same thought when he cautioned the driver of a car to be careful on the slippery street, saying quaintly, "I want to go to glory, but not just yet unless God takes me. There are plenty of good preachers in heaven, but no sinners to reach up there."

Praise God, the Almighty smiles on every faithful believer. He blesses our work, not because we are perfect, but because we are "accepted in the Beloved." Isn't it wonderful to know that we are approved of God! This is because Jesus took our place in death and burial, and we share in His resurrection. The ungodly may say they see no evidence that it makes any difference how we live, but we who have known the joy of being approved of our heavenly Father are happy in the assurance, "God now accepteth thy works."

The Fourth Goad: So Much Is Beyond Man's Control

One of the disturbing aspects of life is the fact that so many things are beyond our control. A person may be self-possessed and confident, regulating closely the affairs of his life as he moves toward his objectives, but an unforeseen blow may throw him off course and render him helpless. He is frustrated because he cannot regulate all facets of his existence. Here is how Solomon describes this situation: "I returned, and saw under the sun, that the race is not to the swift, nor the battle to the strong, neither yet bread to the wise, nor yet riches to men of understanding, nor yet favor to men of skill; but time and chance happeneth to them all. For man also knoweth not his time: like the fish that are taken in an evil net, and like the birds that are caught in the snare, so are the sons of men snared in an evil time, when it falleth suddenly upon them" (Ecc. 9:11-12).

Intelligent people who work hard do not always reach the top of the ladder of success. The fastest runner may be bumped and not win the race. The strongest army may encounter unpredicted elements or be misled by a tactical error and lose the battle. A wise man may be without food because of a natural disaster, and someone with great talent and industry may always be poor because of one setback after another. If one does not reckon with the God of the Bible, he can think humans are like birds which never know when they will be caught in a snare, or fish that might be taken by a net at any instant.

These observations are neither novel nor particularly profound, but they can lead to feelings of fear and hopelessness. Life may not be too depressing for someone who gets a series of "good breaks," but even he will be jolted from time to time when someone smashes into his car or when a loved one dies. We all stand helpless before the unknown and need a source of confidence and understanding beyond ourselves.

The Fourth Nail: The Wise Can Be Influential

The nail of divine revelation given in response might be stated as follows: though some things are beyond your control, the fact remains that a righteous person can greatly influence his world.

The Preacher expresses this idea in a parable. "This wisdom have I seen also under the sun, and it seemed great unto me: there was a little city, and few men within it; and there came a great king against it, and besieged it, and built great bulwarks against it. Now there was found in it a poor wise man, and he, by his wisdom, delivered the city; yet no man remembered that same poor man. Then said I, 'Wisdom is better than strength; nevertheless, the poor man's wisdom is despised, and his words are not heard.' The words of wise men are heard in quiet more than the cry of him that ruleth among fools. Wisdom is better than weapons of war" (Ecc. 9:13-18).

A small city came under attack by a powerful monarch with a well-equipped army. A poor man who possessed wisdom from God directed the defense, and was able to deliver it from the attacking forces. Sadly, when the peril was over, he was quickly forgotten. It remains true, nevertheless, that the wisdom which stems from faith is more powerful than the greatest weapons of modern warfare. The quiet words of a godly man have far more value than the loud pronouncements of an earthly ruler who does not know the Lord.

The person who sees life from the perspective of faith *can* make an impact upon people around him. One such example was related by a young soldier shortly after World War II. Some men of his company occupied a new area during the war and were jubilant because they found a case of liquor in an abandoned building. He was not a Christian at the time and was among the group who planned to join the drinking. But just as the container was about to be opened, a buddy everyone knew was a sincere Christian said, "Fellows, we think we're safe, but there may be enemy troops near us. We don't know what might happen this evening. If you get drunk, we all may be killed. Don't be foolish!"

The officer in charge decided the young man was right and forbade any drinking. It was a good thing he did, for a few hours later the company came under heavy attack. The men were able to fight well and most escaped harm. They should have been thankful that they could act quickly and intelligently, for the good advice of one Christian had saved the entire company from disaster. The man who told the story said he later became a believer because of this Christian soldier's life and witness.

The Preacher then interjects a goadlike thought into this nail section. Godliness is a powerful force, he says, but so is evil. Ecclesiastes 9:18 closes with the words, "But one sinner destroyeth much good." The first verses of chapter 10 point out that the slightest bit of sin can ruin the testimony and good influence of one whose general conduct has been above reproach. "Dead flies cause the ointment of the perfumer to send forth an evil odor; so doth a little folly him that is in reputation for wisdom and honor" (Ecc. 10:1).

When flies fall into precious ointment and die, the perfumed product loses its pleasant scent and becomes repugnant. In the same way, an individual whose high esteem once seemed a sweet fragrance will become odious when he begins to compromise.

The Preacher then says that one who departs from the wisdom of God will not only lose his ability to affect others for good, but will soon become a living testimonial to the foolishness of leaving the way of the Lord. "A wise man's heart is at his right hand, but a fool's heart is at his left. Yea, also, when he that is a fool walketh by the way, his wisdom faileth him, and he saith to every one that he is a fool" (Ecc. 10:2-3).

From this passage some very helpful lessons can be drawn for us today. We can be a great influence for God and truth when we walk in daily dependence upon the Lord and in humble obedience to Him. The power of a Spirit-filled life cannot be overestimated. But every Christian must also be aware of the tremendous danger of compromising with sin. A little too much self-confidence, a small yielding to the flesh, and our testimony can be lost.

What is more pathetic than the sight of a Christian who once radiated joy and gladness as he served the Lord Jesus, but who now limps along as a useless and unhappy misfit because of sin? How relevant the words of the Apostle Paul, "I, therefore, so run, not as uncertainly; so fight I, not as one that beateth the air; but I keep under my body, and bring it into subjection, lest by any means, when I have preached to others, I myself should be a castaway" (1 Cor. 9:26-27).

In conclusion, the man of faith who walks in obedience is among the most blessed people in the world. First, he lives in real joy and assurance, for he knows that all his work and all his relationships have eternal significance. He sees everything as part of God's perfect plan. Second, he is not dismayed in times of adversity and trial. He possesses a deep peace and serenity which is baffling to unbelievers. He knows things are not really the way they sometimes appear, and that God's cause will triumph.

This kind of confidence enabled Samuel Rutherford to write at the top of his letters, "God's Palace, Aberdeen" while he was imprisoned in a dungeon.

A similar assurance gave the well-educated and cultured Madame Guyon the ability to manifest joy while spending 10 long years in confinement. She wrote, "While I was a prisoner in Vincennes, I passed my time in great peace. I sang songs of joy which a maid who served me learned by heart as fast as I made them. And we together sang Thy praises, O my God. The stones of my prison walls shone like rubies in my eyes. My heart was full of that joy which Thou givest to them that love Thee in the midst of their greatest crosses."

Even though locked up in a dungeon she was spiritually triumphant, and wrote a beautiful hymn to express the personal victory she experienced as she viewed life with the perspective of faith.

A little bird am I,
Shut out from fields of air,
Yet in my cage I sit and sing
To Him who placed me there.
Well pleased a prisoner to be,
Because, my God, it pleaseth Thee.

Naught else have I to do,
I sing the whole day long,
And He whom I love most to please
Dost listen to my song.
He caught and bound my wandering wing,
But still He bends to hear me sing.

My cage confines me 'round,
Abroad I cannot fly,
But though my wings are closely bound,
My heart's at liberty.
My prison walls cannot control
The flight, the freedom of the soul.

Oh, it is good to soar
These bolts and bars above,
To Him whose purpose I adore,
Whose providence I love,
And in Thy mighty will to find
The joy, the freedom of the mind.

Yes, how wonderfully true the words of the Apostle John, "And this is the victory that overcometh the world, even our faith" (1 John 5:4).

11
Here Comes the Judges' Judge

In 1815, when Napoleon was at the zenith of his power, his armies were unexpectedly defeated by the allies under the command of Wellington. A heavy rain throughout the night before the fateful battle made the roads of Waterloo so soft that Napoleon could not carry out his plans. He had hoped to have his artillery booming at the break of dawn, but as it was, the large guns could not be drawn into position until almost noon. This delay enabled Wellington's troops to hold the French at bay until the arrival of massive Prussian reinforcements turned the tide of battle.

A writer commenting upon the unusual and unexpected downpour made the statement, "A cloud traversing the sky out of season sufficed to make a world crumble."

The great novelist Victor Hugo wrote, "Why was Napoleon defeated? Because of his own mistakes? Because of Wellington's superior forces? No! Because of God!"

Victor Hugo was right. God's patience with a

cruel and unjust government comes to an end, and His judgment falls. The history of the Lord's dealings with the nations bears out this truth.

As an example, God told Abraham that when the iniquity of the Amorites "was full," He would drive them out of the land and bring in the Israelites. So He did, under Moses centuries later.

God revealed to the Prophet Habakkuk that the Babylonians, the instrument of God for the judgment of Judah's sins, would themselves be punished for their cruelty. In prophecy the Lord said of the Babylonian empire, "Because thou hast spoiled many nations, all the remnant of the peoples shall spoil thee, because of men's blood, and for the violence of the land, of the city, and of all that dwell therein" (Hab. 2:8).

God will not permit cruel, oppressive, and immoral empires to endure unchecked. He normally does not overthrow them by miraculous raining of fire from heaven or some other spectacular judgment, but by natural disasters, war, and internal decay. The empires of Egypt, Assyria, Babylon, Persia, Greece, and Rome all rose to prominence through the might of arms, flourished for a season, and then collapsed in defeat. In every instance a major factor leading to their downfall was their selfish greed and gross immorality, first infecting the leaders and gradually spreading to include the general population.

This theme, that the Lord will use weakness of godless rulers to bring about the end of their domain, is developed in Ecclesiastes 10:4-20. Believers in God who are forced to live in a society where evil, atheistic men are in power can find great encouragement and instruction in these words of the Preacher. In fact, it is said that the Jews who suffered under the domination of Persia found much hope and assurance in this passage. They identified with the circumstances described here, and rejoiced in the prospect of a sure deliverance.

Following a realistic warning to believers to wait upon God rather than joining impetuously in a hasty revolt (v. 4), Solomon portrays a godless empire as having everything upside down and out of joint. He then gives a number of reasons a child of God can remain hopeful in the face of a distressing political environment and concludes with a series of practical exhortations for living a successful Christian life under these circumstances.

A Goad: Society Is Out of Order

The inspired writer portrays social or political conditions that seem to be all wrong. From the very top authority in government down through every rung on the ladder of society, things are not as they should be. "There is an evil which I have seen under the sun, as an error which proceedeth from the ruler: folly is set in great dignity, and the rich sit in low place. I have seen servants upon horses, and princes walking like servants upon the earth" (Ecc. 10:5-7).

This is what happens when dishonest or unscrupulous men control a country. A careful look at the text shows that the "servants" are placed in juxtaposition to those he personifies as "folly." Therefore, the "rich" and the "princes" in this portrayal represent people who possess true wisdom and godliness. On the other hand, the men in the positions of authority, riding grandly on horses, are "fools" who do not deserve to rule.

Solomon does not tell us how this developed. It is not his purpose to give a specific example, but to indicate the reversal of God's social order, the condition that falls upon a nation when it is ruled by unqualified and evil men. Their lack of true wisdom and tendency toward selfishness and bad judgment cause much injustice and suffering. The righteous are oppressed, the innocent endure hardship, and morality and holiness are ignored. But the believer is not to give up hope, for God's way will prevail.

A Nail: Wicked Rulers Are in Jeopardy

Having pictured the unhealthy political situation under the rule of evil men, Solomon proceeds in verses 8-11 to set forth a number of reasons why they will not hold power indefinitely. He does so by the use of a series of proverbs: expressions from everyday life to teach moral truths. Their meaning is determined by the general context. The verses immediately preceding and following this passage talk about living under wicked governments.

Solomon presents the first basic truth by putting two sayings together. One concerns a trapper who catches wild animals in pits, and the other, a workman who tears down a stone hedge. "He that diggeth a pit shall fall into it; and whoso breaketh an hedge, a serpent shall bite him" (Ecc. 10:8).

The truth of these maxims is the same as our modern saying, "If you play with fire, you're going to be burned." The hunter might forget the location of one of his pits and fall into it, and the man destroying a wall may be bitten by a viper hiding in one of the crannies. Even so, cruel and unjust rulers put themselves in jeopardy by their very acts of tyranny. People will endure excessively severe treatment only so long before striking back, and the oppressor will finally be bitten by the fury of an angered populace.

The second truth is also presented by two epigrams. When men break stones with sledge-hammers, or split timbers with axes, they may be injured by flying splinters in the process. "Whoso removeth stones shall be hurt therewith; and he that splitteth wood shall be endangered thereby (Ecc. 10:9).

Quarrying rock and milling lumber are constructive activities, and therefore this adage may indicate that even when a godless ruler tries to bring some benefits to his people, he will encounter dangers. A few good projects cannot overshadow the general corruption of his government, and the subjected citizenry will not be fooled. They may still revolt when the opportunity occurs.

The third maxim depicts a man working with a dull axe or knife. He expends a great deal of time and energy to accomplish very little. If he were wise, he would sharpen the tool so that he could do the task more effectively. "If the iron be blunt, and he do not whet the edge, then must he put forth more strength, but wisdom is profitable to direct" (Ecc. 10:10).

An empire, ruler, or political organization that leaves out God is like this foolish workman. Whenever leaders lack the true wisdom that comes from Jehovah, they are doomed to great difficulty and frustration.

The next proverb declares that a person who gives heed to one who talks foolishly puts himself in serious jeopardy. "Surely the serpent will bite without enchantment, and a babbler is no better" (Ecc. 10:11). Just as a poisonous snake brings grave danger to one unskilled in handling it, so a babbler is dangerous and treacherous, a threat to everyone.

By way of application, this axiom says that a monarch who does not receive the divine enablement available through prayer will not be able to rule successfully. His subjects will turn on him, for they are sinners just as he is. The sin principle, which infects the whole human race, is so powerful that no earthly ruler can maintain control without the Lord's help.

Furthermore, the ruler only harms himself by consulting those who would give unsound or nonsensical advice. All efforts of the "babblers," or false prophets, will be in vain, for they are unable to put a man in touch with the true and living God.

The step from *enchantment* in the proverb to *prayer* in the application is not nearly as long as it may appear. The Hebrew word in the saying is the same term used to denote prayer in other Scriptures. It occurs, for example, in Isaiah 26:16 where the prophet says, "Lord, in trouble have they visited Thee; they poured out a *prayer* when Thy chastening was upon them." That the *babbler* refers to a false prophet is indicated by the Hebrew term—*ba'al hallashon*—which literally means "master of the tongue." When used in an unfavorable manner as it is here, it denotes a deceiver.

The evil and prayerless ruler, who heeds the unsound advice of magicians, soothsayers, or other ungodly "babblers," is in danger of falling. His reliance upon their idle chatter will lead him to serious errors and a weakened rule.

A Nail: The Godless Will Not
Realize Their Ambitions

Still writing against the background of the political

evils portrayed earlier in this chapter, the Preacher declares that wicked men will not reach all their goals, for the lack of true wisdom augurs their failure. They are flouting God's laws, and whenever anyone does this, he becomes more and more enmeshed in the consequences of his own blunders. This is true of all proud and arrogant men, but the context seems to relate these words especially to rulers of nations. "The words of a wise man's mouth are gracious, but the lips of a fool will swallow up himself. The beginning of the words of his mouth is foolishness, and the end of his talk is mischievous madness" (Ecc. 10:12-13).

What a contrast between the words of a godly man and the pompous expressions of a proud monarch! By the use of Hebrew parallelism, the "gracious" expressions of the believer are set against the vain statements of the foolish ruler. He will "swallow himself up" by his own thoughtless words and unwise remarks, for they will lead to his undoing.

This passage brings to mind the arrogance and incredible idiocy combined in Adolf Hitler. During the time he was proclaiming his doctrine of Aryan supremacy and whipping up his public to cries of *"Heil Hitler! Deutschland über alles!"* he was the personification of self-conceit and swagger. But later, when he insisted upon final say in military matters, a series of unbelievable blunders on his part enabled the allied armies to overrun his country and defeat him.

How true of Hitler and others like him are the Preacher's statements, "A fool also is full of words. A man cannot tell what shall be; and what shall be after him, who can tell him? The labor of the foolish wearieth every one of them, because he knoweth not how to go to the city" (Ecc. 10:14-15).

Unqualified men in high positions are filled with a false bravado because they do not know what will happen to them. In actuality they are often short-sighted and subject to delusions, and Solomon compares them to a man who can not even follow the road signs to the city. Today we would say that they don't know enough to come in out of the rain.

How can we account for the fact that intelligent men with well-established success patterns in business or professional life make glaring errors in judgment when they gain political power? Three factors may be cited as explanations. First, men easily become blinded by their own sinful pride. People in the public eye are particularly suscep-tible to this danger. Second, they surround them-selves with self-seeking advisors who give faulty counsel. Third, they are often deluded by cruel, wicked spirits under the rule of Satan.

The Old Testament tells us that Ahab, an idolatrous king of Israel, was led to his death on the battlefield by advice which actually came from an evil spirit. The king had been warned by the Prophet Micaiah that his personal advisors and prophets, who strongly urged him to go into battle, were speaking under the influence of a "lying spirit." "Now, therefore, behold, the Lord hath put a lying spirit in the mouth of all these thy prophets, and the Lord hath spoken evil concerning thee" (1 Kings 22:23).

This does not mean that messengers of Satan operate under the direct command of God. The Lord maintains ultimate control of all things, and He *allows* wicked spirits to lead kings and nations into disaster.

The same truth is also set forth in the Book of Revelation. The beloved apostle tells of three unclean spirits "that go forth unto kings of the earth and of the whole world, to gather them to the battle of that great day of God Almighty" (Rev. 16:14). These demons will impel the rebellious rulers of nations to undertake a foolhardy expedition against God, and disaster will fall upon them. Apparently these followers of Satan take fiendish delight in leading men to certain defeat.

Christians living in countries where they are not permitted to worship in public or openly tell the story of Jesus can rest assured that the oppressive regime will not always continue. It will not achieve its ultimate purposes! It will be cast down by its own inadequacy and the intervening hand of God.

A Nail: Debauchery Insures Defeat

The Preacher gives yet another reason why God's children who are forced to live under a tyrannical or unjust government may be assured of its downfall. Whenever a governing faction is entrenched in power and feels secure, its leaders succumb to the temptations of the flesh. Flagrant immorality begins to manifest itself in high places.

Solomon says that such rulers are as irresponsible as little children, thinking only of themselves. All their thoughts, even their first ones in the morning, are of self-indulgence rather than the solemn affairs of government. "Woe to thee, O land, when thy king is a child, and thy princes eat in the morning! Blessed art thou, O land, when thy king is the son of nobles, and thy princes eat in due season, for strength, and not for drunkenness! By much slothfulness the building decayeth, and through idleness of the hands the house droppeth through" (Ecc. 10: 16-18).

History has repeatedly confirmed the truth of these verses. Power in the hands of godless men works toward the deterioration of character. Idealism fades, affairs of government are neglected, and temperance is forgotten. It is not long before such leaders lose their position of authority. Why? Because God has established moral law, and He will not allow anyone to break His commandments with impunity. These laws are written into the very fabric of the universe and the fiber of men, and will not be denied.

A Word of Counsel: Respect Authority

The Preacher continues with some works of general advice applicable to all people. Since they follow so closely his statements about evil rulers, they very likely have special meaning for those who live in circumstances marked by gross injustice.

The first admonition is a warning against seditious thoughts and words. "Curse not the king, no, not in thy thought; and curse not the rich in thy bedchamber; for a bird of the air shall carry the voice, and that which hath wings shall tell the matter" (Ecc. 10:20).

It is never right to harbor hatred against a leader, nor is it proper to make slanderous statements. This may be especially dangerous when one lives under the rule of a dictator. Even the walls sometimes seem to have ears, and the way one's remarks reach people for whom they were not intended make it seem as if the birds of the air are tattlers.

When a dictator and his associates are gradually losing power and feel that their influence is slipping, they often tend to become increasingly suspicious and paranoid. Long before modern "bugging" techniques were instituted, leaders had ways of finding out what people were saying. In fascist and Marxist countries, for example, husbands and wives have sometimes betrayed one another, and children have spoken against their parents. Besides, one never knows when an inadvertent remark might be picked up and given a wrong connotation. Then too in an atmosphere of suspicion, revolutionary remarks are not only dangerous but also ineffective. A person can get himself killed and accomplish nothing by it.

These warnings about dictators may seem irrelevant to you if you have always lived under a democracy. But you have no guarantee that you will always have your freedom. In today's world, changes can occur rapidly. A dictatorship can regiment people more effectively than at any time in history because of the advances of technology and the speed by which men can communicate.

In all situations, the biblical pattern calls for submission to authority in every area that does not violate God's laws and the Christian conscience. Only when obedience to man means disobedience to God should one resist. The Apostle Paul declared, "Let every soul be subject unto the higher powers. For there is no power but of God; the powers that be are ordained of God" (Rom. 13:1).

The first-century Christians left us a good example. They lived under varying degrees of persecution by the Roman government, but did not lead riots or stir up rebellious movements. Only when ordered to offer incense to Caesar and thus attribute deity to him did they refuse to obey the authorities. Then they willingly suffered for Christ's sake.

Further Counsel: Do Good to Others

The second admonition of the Preacher is a call for godly action. This, of course, is applicable at any time. In days of prosperity and freedom, even believers in Christ are inclined to become self-centered and worldly; under degenerative conditions they are apt to sit back and wait for better days, doing nothing more constructive than complaining. The Preacher therefore issues a positive commandment: "Cast thy bread upon the waters; for thou shalt find it after many days. Give a portion to seven, and also to eight; for thou knowest not what evil shall be upon the earth" (Ecc. 11: 1-2).

These unusual words can be understood best if we think of sending a ship out to sea loaded with good things for others. Solomon may have had in mind the vessels he used in trade with King Hiram. This fleet would embark on a three-year voyage throughout the Mediterranean, and return with a rich cargo of gold, silver, ivory, apes, and peacocks (see 1 Kings 10:22). Similarly, when we give freely to others, we may be sure of a bountiful return. Kindness and sacrificial giving is always pleasing to the Lord, but especially so in unsettling times.

Solomon's call for benevolent activity is followed by a warning against hasty action. He says, "If the clouds be full of rain, they empty themselves upon the earth; and if the tree fall toward the south, or toward the north, in the place where the tree falleth, there it shall be" (Ecc. 11:3).

Just as men do not have to do anything to make the rain fall from water-filled clouds, so we must sometimes wait for God to act rather than taking things into our own hands. This has a special application to people living under wicked conditions.

Believers do not need to instigate open rebellion, for God will bring haughty men low in His own time. The inspired writer uses the symbolism of trees, as is done so often throughout the Old Testament, to depict the fate of earthly rulers and their empires when God sends them crashing to the ground.

Then, too, no one should be so totally occupied with current trends or speculations of impending changes that he fails in his responsibility to do the work God has given him. Solomon declares, "He that observeth the wind shall not sow, and he that regardeth the clouds shall not reap. As thou knowest not what is the way of the wind, nor how the bones grow in the womb of her who is with child, even so thou knowest not the works of God, who maketh all. In the morning sow thy seed, and in the evening withhold not thine hand; for thou knowest not which shall prosper, either this or that, or whether they both shall be alike good" (Ecc. 11: 4-6).

The Apostle Paul issued an injunction to Christians which beautifully supplements Solomon's admonition. "Therefore, my beloved brethren, be ye steadfast, unmovable, always abounding in the work of the Lord, forasmuch as ye know that your labor is not in vain in the Lord" (1 Cor. 15:58).

To summarize, these words of the Preacher are a source of rich encouragement and instruction to all believers. Though the context seems to indicate that they are addressed in a special way to people living under the reign of evil rulers, they contain truths applicable to everyone. Christians who can say, "The lines are fallen unto me in pleasant places," should not forget the multitudes who live in countries where poverty, persecution, and suppression of liberty are the daily lot of those who love the Lord Jesus. Let us pray for them, and thank God for the assurance that the powers of evil are certain to fall.

Finally, the believer need never go down the dead-end street of worry and fruitlessness. No matter how terrible the conditions of the society in which he lives, he can trust God for the future. He can obey the admonition, "Cast thy bread upon the waters" with a confident heart, knowing it will return. He can rejoice in this assurance whenever he does good to his fellowmen in the name of Christ, and especially as he presents the Gospel of salvation.

Adoniram Judson labored diligently and sacrificially for seven long years before making one convert, but later saw a multitude of souls come to Christ.

Francis Booth Tucker, who left an important government position to minister for Christ in India, worked faithfully for many years and suffered much without apparent results. Finally, however, thousands came to the Saviour through his diligent efforts.

Paul declared, "He who soweth bountifully shall reap also bountifully" (2 Cor. 9:6). If you will scatter an abundance of words and deeds for your Master, you will reap a rich harvest—if not on earth, certainly in heaven. Wicked men and their empires can endure for only a little while, but to Christians the Bible gives the wonderful assurances that "he that doeth the will of God abideth forever" (1 John 2:17) and "their works do follow them" (Rev. 14:13).

12

The Highway to Happiness

God intends that His children have a rich, rewarding, and joy-filled life. The man who joined the church saying, "Here's to a miserable life on earth with heaven at the end," did not have a proper concept of Christianity. Faith in Christ gives freedom to the soul, fills the heart with light, and puts a song upon the lips.

Of course, this does not mean that every believer will always wear a broad smile or feel like laughing. It would be wrong to imply that all who believe in the Lord will be successful in each undertaking, enjoy continuous glowing health, and be free from all care and sorrow. On the contrary, the most devout believer may live in grinding poverty, suffer physical maladies, or be forced to endure crushing disappointment and deep grief.

The happiness of the Christian does not depend upon happenings. Through his faith in the Word of God, he possesses a deep inner peace which triumphs over circumstances. This can bring him real satisfaction, enrich his every earthly joy, and give him strength for every burden, whatever it may be.

The closing section of Ecclesiastes marks out the pathway to this good life. It exhorts young people to relish the wholesome pleasures of youth, urges them to give God His rightful place, admonishes believers to honor and obey the Bible, and summarizes the living message of the entire book.

Delight in Legitimate Pleasure

How wonderful to be young! God desires that these exuberant and carefree days be filled with happiness. But let every young person keep in mind that he is a moral and spiritual being responsible to God for his conduct. "Rejoice, O young man, in thy youth, and let thy heart cheer thee in the days of thy youth, and walk in the ways of thine heart, and in the sight of thine eyes; but know thou, that for all these things God will bring thee into judgment. Therefore, remove sorrow from thy heart, and put away evil from thy flesh; for childhood and youth are vanity" (Ecc. 11:9-10).

The inspired writer encourages the young person to "walk in the ways of thy heart, and in the sight of thine eyes." Taken by itself, this admonition could be interpreted as a directive to obey every impulse, righteous or sinful. This is not what the Preacher had in mind, however, for he immediately adds, "But know thou, that for all these things God will bring thee into judgment."

Even in youth one must view life as a whole. He must realize that his time on earth is only the prelude to eternity. He dares not take the view of a skeptic about whom my father, Dr. M. R. De Haan, wrote. The man scoffed, "I'm not concerned about the future. I live for today and let tomorrow take care of itself. I follow the words of Solomon, 'Rejoice, O young man, in thy youth.' My song is, 'In the Sweet Here and Now.'"

My father commented as follows: "If this is your philosophy of life, you are being foolish. A successful man doesn't do business that way! He has a sense of perspective—he thinks ahead to tomorrow. His activities today are definitely related to his plans for next week, next month, and even next year.

"In the spiritual the same is true. No intelligent man going on a trip into an unknown region will start without careful planning. He will consult road maps and read every travel folder he can find for prior information. But thousands of people are so unwise that even though they know a *long* eternity awaits them, and they sometimes have disquieting thoughts about coming judgment, their only interest is the 'here and now.'"

If you are searching for true happiness, you must obtain peace of mind regarding the days of reckoning to come after you die. Otherwise even the pleasure of the moment is marred by the underlying realization that you as a sinner are living daily under the sentence of death and awaiting execution.

Never forget that God designed you to live a holy, happy life in fellowship with Him. As long as you are alienated from the Lord, you are under the shadow of condemnation. You cannot fulfill the purpose for which He created you. Augustine was right when he penned in his famous *Confessions*, "Thou madest us for Thyself, and we shall never find rest save as we rest in Thee." You can know true happiness only through faith in Jesus Christ.

Having warned young people to include in their equation of life the awareness that "God will bring

thee into judgment," the Preacher goes on to tell
them how they can legitimately enjoy their youth.
He says, "Remove sorrow from thy heart, and put
away evil from thy flesh." In this twofold admonition Solomon is saying that the young should not
give themselves over to sadness, and that they
should avoid physical distresses.

The expression, "put away evil from thy flesh" is
not primarily a warning against sins of lust, but is
advice not to suffer pain unnecessarily. This is indicated both by the context and by the use of the
Hebrew word *ra'ah*, which denotes physical and
material calamity or misfortune. In Isaiah 45:7, for
example, God declares, "I make peace, and create
evil [*ra'ah*]." This obviously refers to the hardship
and suffering He brings as a consequence of sin.
In view of this, we believe Solomon is urging
young people to do what they can to enjoy the
vigor and strength that are unique to this stage of
life. He is also warning them that if they abuse or
harm their bodies while young, they will have to
pay the consequences the rest of their lives.

At first glance, these instructions may not seem
to be particularly relevant to today's young people.
Most may be inclined to sin more in the direction
of excessive frivolity and carnality than in self-
affliction, such as is done by the "holy men" of
India. These words do have value, nevertheless, for
they sanction the wholesome pleasures of youth,
and indicate that they can be experienced without
feelings of guilt.

The Almighty reveals clearly in His Word that
He is pleased with the laughter of children and the
special joys of the young. In Zechariah's graphic
portrayal of Jerusalem during the millennial age,
we read, "And the streets of the city shall be full

of boys and girls playing" (Zech. 8:5). In fact, the Bible frequently praises the strength and beauty of young manhood and womanhood.

After encouraging the young to enjoy the legitimate pleasures of their carefree years, the Preacher concludes with the statement, "Childhood and youth are vanity." These words are not to be taken as minimizing this period of life, but as declaring that its freshness and vigor will not last very long. Therefore its joys must not be considered an end in themselves. Delight in youth, but do not overlook the whole picture, including judgment and eternity.

The wisdom of young people enjoying life within the limits of their consciousness of God's will and coming judgment has been proven in experience. A happy childhood is a vital factor in the development of a well-balanced life. Those who are given a stable environment and cultivate a joyful heart while they are in these formative years more than likely will be cheerful people through all their days. The one who has learned to trust God in youth, and from this step of faith has acquired an optimistic outlook, will undoubtedly be victorious when trials come. True, we must walk with the Lord on a day-to-day basis, but the person who has learned to do this in childhood has a great advantage over the one who must begin a life of faith in later years.

When we grow older, our bodies may become pain-wracked and weary, our minds baffled by adverse circumstances, and our hearts saddened by losses, but our steadfast faith, which dates from childhood and has stood the test of the years, will enable us to rise above them all. In times of adversity God often brings verses of Scripture to our memories that we learned as children. The songs of devotion we lifted so sincerely when we were young run through our minds again. By these we are spiritually sustained.

Remember God While Young

The Preacher's second exhortation is to give God the strength and vitality of our youthful days. "Remember now thy Creator in the days of thy youth, while the evil days come not, nor the years draw near when thou shalt say, 'I have no pleasure in them'; while the sun, or the light, or the moon, or the stars, are not darkened, nor the clouds return after the rain" (Ecc. 12:1-2).

The call to place God and His will uppermost in your thinking during childhood stands in sharp contrast to the philosophy of many. All too often people say they will sow their wild oats in their youth and then turn over the rest of their lives to the Lord. They have the idea that in this way they can enjoy the best of this life and still enter heaven.

This attitude is wrong, first of all, because it is an insult to the Lord. He deserves and asks nothing less than our best. A woman named Mrs. Mack once taught an attractive young lady this lesson in a unique manner. She sent the girl a box of roses so wilted that their petals were falling. The girl was surprised to receive the gift and bewildered when she saw the condition of the flowers, but she passed it off with the thought that perhaps their delivery had been delayed because of an oversight.

Later that day she met Mrs. Mack on the street and thanked her for the roses. The older woman smiled and said, "I'm glad you liked them. I cut them last Monday and enjoyed them all week, but this morning when I noticed they were beginning to get old and faded, I thought of you and had them delivered to your door."

Seeing the puzzled and hurt look on the girl's face, she continued, "The other evening I was sitting in the car while my husband went into the drugstore. As you walked by, I heard you telling someone that you were going to become a Christian later, not while you are still young. You said you wanted to have a good time first. How selfish! You wish to give the Lord your life after the beauty, charm, and vigor have faded, and you have become old and wrinkled. I thought these roses would illustrate what you are doing to the Lord by waiting."

The girl learned the lesson of the wilted flowers and soon accepted Christ and began to serve Him with zeal.

A second reason for remembering the Creator in youth is this: a life of obedience and devotion to God is the only way to lasting happiness. When a young person combines the enthusiasm, idealism, and energy of youth with a deep devotion to the Lord, he has all the ingredients for a wonderful life. Free from feelings of guilt and fear, he is at peace with himself, God, and the world. He experiences a sense of fulfillment as he does the will of God, and looks forward to a lifetime of joyous service followed by eternal glory with his Saviour.

The inspired author emphasizes his plea to remember God early in life by portraying the contrast between youth and old age. When we are young, the sun, moon, and stars shine brightly in an unclouded sky, but as we near the end of the road everything is different.

In figurative terminology the Preacher pictures an aged man as standing at the door of death. "In the day when the keepers of the house shall tremble, and the strong men shall bow themselves, and the grinders cease because they are few, and those that look out of the windows are darkened, and the doors shall be shut in the streets; when the sound of the grinding is low, and he shall rise up at the voice of the bird, and all the daughters of music shall be brought low; also when they shall be afraid of that which is high, and fears shall be in the way, and the almond tree shall flourish, and the grasshopper shall be a burden, and desire shall fail; because man goeth to his long home, and the mourners go about the streets" (Ecc. 12:3-5).

Bible students have gone to great lengths to find deep spiritual meanings for these highly descriptive phrases. But most likely it is best to see them as only a portrayal of the marks of extreme age. The "keepers of the house" are the arms which shake; the "strong men" are the legs which become bowed; the "grinders" are the teeth which are few in number; "those that look out of the windows" are the eyes which are dimmed by the passing years, and the "doors" are the ears which can barely hear the grinding of grain, a daily occurrence in an oriental home. The expression "he shall rise up at the sound of the bird" indicates that the aged person can no longer sleep well. He is awakened by the first singing birds of the morning, even though he can hardly hear their music.

The author further depicts the old man as being "afraid of that which is high." This could mean that he is fearful of doing anything involving climbing, for he knows his wobbly legs will have difficulty supporting him. He is also apprehensive about walking along a path, for he is no longer agile and stumbles easily. The reference to the almond tree perhaps describes the silver locks which adorn the

aged person's head, and the mention of the grasshopper, which has a hesitant, dragging gait when it
walks, might be intended to portray the shuffling,
stooped carriage of the elderly as they move along.
The expression "desire shall fail" points up the fact
that physical appetites have waned and bodily
functions have slowed. Death is imminent. The
aged man will soon "go to his long home," entering
into his eternal state, and then the hired mourners
will begin their loud lamentations.

The words "or ever," which open verse 6, refer
back to the beginning of this section. They are a
call to remember God before "the silver cord is
loosed, or the golden bowl is broken, or the pitcher
is broken at the fountain, or the wheel broken at
the cistern" (see Ecc. 12:6.)

Some commentators relate these descriptive
terms of the Preacher to specific parts of the body.
One leading scholar, for example, makes the golden
bowl to be the head, the silver cord the spinal col-
umn, the pitcher the blood vessels, the fountain the
right ventricle of the heart, the cistern the left ventricle, and the wheel the aorta.

It seems best not to press these images that far,
however. They more likely are intended to set forth
the truths that life is precious, its tenure is uncertain, and its inevitable end is death. As the severing
of the silver cord causes the valuable golden lamp
to be smashed, so death cuts off the precious gift of
life. As a fragile pitcher must be handled carefully
so that it is not allowed to swing against the side
of the tile fountain and break, so man is frail and
may die at any time from even minor causes. As
the wheel used to lower vessels into a deep cistern
is a mechanical contrivance bound to deteriorate,
so the human body must finally wear out.

Solomon's portrayal of old age is admittedly very dismal. Most people die before all these evidences of physical breakdown become noticeable. Yet this is an accurate picture of what happens when one reaches an advanced age, and the Preacher has accomplished his purpose in warning young people to serve God while they possess strength and vitality.

Some Bible students have said that this description can be applied only to the sensualist, not to the godly. They support their contention by quoting promises such as, "The righteous shall flourish like the palm tree. . . . they shall still bring forth fruit in old age" (Ps. 92:12, 14). But this is not a guarantee believers are immune from the general physical infirmities of the aged. Even so, the Christian need not be disheartened. He can still be joyous in spirit.

Put God's Word First

As Solomon brings Ecclesiastes to its climax, he returns to his opening theme, gives a resumé of what he did in writing the book, and issues a strong admonition to place the highest priority upon the inspired words of Scripture. "Vanity of vanities, saith the Preacher; all is vanity. And, moreover, because the Preacher was wise, he still taught the people knowledge; yea, he gave good heed, and sought out, and set in order many proverbs. The Preacher sought to find out acceptable words; and that which was written was upright, even words of truth. The words of the wise are like goads; and like nails fastened by the masters of assemblies, which are given by one Shepherd. And further, by these, my son, be admonished: of making many books there is no end; and much study is a weariness of the flesh" (Ecc. 12:8-12).

The Preacher exhorts his readers to accept the counsel of this book he has written. He seems to be aware of its unique inspiration as part of the sacred Scriptures, for he sets it in opposition to the many literary productions of his day. Notice his words, "And, further, by *these*, my son, be admonished." This is an obvious reference to the "acceptable words," the "words of truth," the "nails . . . which are given by one Shepherd" of verses 10 and 11. We should therefore heed God's Word and not the "many books," which produce only "weariness of the flesh" in those who study them.

The Preacher is certainly not saying that the Bible is the only volume worth reading. But this we do know, that when men try to answer questions about God and eternity in their own wisdom, they wander in circles and finally wind up on a dead-end street. How wonderful that we can go to the Bible, knowing that it contains authentic and inspired information to guide us through time into eternity! Not books, but *the Book!*

Fear God and Obey Him

The final words of the Preacher are an explicit command, and they summarize the entire message of Ecclesiastes. He says, "Fear God, and keep His commandments; for this is the whole duty of man" (Ecc. 12:13).

Solomon presents two strong reasons we should live in reverential awe of God and obedience to Him. The first is expressed in the words "this is the whole duty of man." Notice that the word *duty* is italicized in the King James Version, which means that it has been added by the translators. It makes good sense as rendered here, and this may be exactly what the Preacher had in mind.

Some Hebrew scholars, however, have translated this phrase, "This is for *all* men." It thus becomes an affirmation that reverence and obedience is the duty of everyone. This version is also in harmony with Scripture, and therefore might be accepted as a reasonable alternative.

Many textual authorities prefer the translation, "This is the *whole* man." They believe these words are saying that man reaches the full ideal for which God created him when he lives in the fear of God and keeps His commandments. The Lord made man that he might glorify Him and enjoy Him forevermore. Man fulfills that purpose when he is right with God!

The second reason for living in reverential awe and obedience to God is the truth that at some future time everyone must meet Him at the judgment bar. "For God shall bring every work into judgment, with every secret thing, whether it be good, or whether it be evil" (Ecc. 12:14).

In that day, every sin, even the deepest thoughts of the heart, will be brought to light and judged. An electronic machine known as a spectrophotometer uses ultraviolet rays to examine the most minute particles of matter—solid, gas, or liquid. In 15 minutes it can provide a complete analysis of their composition! But the performance of this amazing device is nothing compared to the perceptive power of the eye of God. He looks upon your life and mine and sees even the hidden motives that underlie our words and actions. We must never forget that "all things are naked and opened unto the eyes of Him with whom we have to do" (Heb. 4:13). What an awesome thought!

Are you prepared for your appointment with the Judge of the universe? If not, get ready today. Life is uncertain. The Bible says, "All have sinned, and come short of the glory of God" (Rom. 3:23), and, "The wages of sin is death" (Rom. 6:23). But it also says, "For God so loved the world, that he gave His only begotten Son, that whosoever believeth in Him should not perish, but have everlasting life" (John 3:16).

If you have never placed your trust in Him, bow your head right now and utter this simple prayer of faith: "Lord Jesus, I know I am a sinner who deserves Your wrath. I believe You died to pay for my sins, and that You arose from the dead. I am receiving You now as my Saviour, my only hope of salvation. Save me. I do believe. Amen." When you do, you can then claim the promise, "Whosoever shall call upon the name of the Lord shall be saved" (Rom. 10:13).

Conclusion

The Book of Ecclesiastes was written by a man who truly believed in Jehovah. It depicts in graphic detail the dead-end streets of attempting to solve life's deepest problems in one's own wisdom. Writing from personal experience and observation, Solomon has demonstrated the futility of trying to arrive at final answers through the study of nature or human philosophy. He has depicted the blind alleys of pleasure, fame, material accomplishment. Man's best efforts, he has proven, fall short of achieving happiness.

Since God has revealed Himself and His way in the Bible, however, a true believer can view the perplexities, injustices, and sorrows of life without despair, for he knows the Lord has a good plan. He realizes the perils of wealth and fame, and avoids these avenues by which many become enmeshed in tangled webs of dishonesty and deceit. He can enjoy to the full the zestful, vibrant days of youth, for he is confident that the fear of God and obedience to His commandments bring the joy of divine approval.

The writer of Ecclesiastes has clearly revealed that two contrasting roads lie before man. One is a dead-end street, for it takes man into the labyrinth of his own futile efforts. The other is the way of perfect wisdom. It follows the truth of God as revealed in the Bible. The choice is yours.

Perhaps you have discovered that life is not always easy. You have been through many difficult experiences and confronted baffling enigmas. These have acted as painful goads, pricking your mind and conscience. But they will have served their purpose if they drive you to the nails of truth in God's revelation. By faith in Him you can stay off the fog-shrouded maze of dead-end streets, and walk the clearly marked road to everlasting life.